COUNTRY WALKS AROUND HARROGATE

Volume 1 East

by

Douglas Cossar

for

The Ramblers' Association West Riding Area
(www.ramblersyorkshire.org)

Other publications by the Ramblers' Association (West Riding Area)

Kiddiwalks (2005)
Douglas Cossar, *Ramblers' Leeds, vol. 1 East (1999)*
Douglas Cossar, *Ramblers' Leeds, vol. 2 West (2000)*
Douglas Cossar, *Ramblers' Bradford (1999)*
Douglas Cossar, *The Wakefield Way (2004)*
Douglas Cossar, The Airedale Way (1996)
Douglas Cossar & John Lieberg, *Country Walks in Mirfield, Emley, Thornhill and Denby Dale (2007)*
Dales Way Handbook (with the Dales Way Association, annually)

© Ramblers' Association 2007

ISBN 978-1-906494-02-5

Printed by Hart & Clough Ltd, Cleckheaton

Cover photographs. Front: ford at Lime Kilns Farm (Walk 17)
Back: Kirkby Overblow; viaduct on the former Leeds-Thirsk railway; Devil's Arrows
All photographs by Keith Wadd.

Publishers' Note
At the time of publication all footpaths used in these walks were designated as public rights of way or permissive footpaths, but it should be borne in mind that diversion orders may be made from time to time. Although every care has been taken in the preparation of this guide, the publishers cannot accept responsibility for those who stray from the routes described.

Contents

Introduction... 5

1. Weeton and Rougemont.. 9

2. Harewood Park.. 12

3. Clap Gate and Barrowby... 14

4. Spofforth and Sicklinghall... 16

5. Spofforth to Kirkby Overblow...................................... 17

6. Pannal to Kirkby Overblow... 20

7. Follifoot and Crimple Beck... 24

8. Rudding Park and the Crimple Valley.......................... 26

9. Knaresborough, Plompton, Ribston and Goldsborough ... 30

10. Hay-a-Park and Coneythorpe................................ 34

11. Whixley and Allerton Mauleverer................................ 37

12. Tockwith riverside.. 40

13. The Nidd Gorge... 41

14. Staveley and Copgrove.. 44

15. Boroughbridge and Aldborough.................................. 46

16. Burton Leonard and Bishop Monkton.......................... 49

17. South Stainley, Burton Leonard and Brearton.............. 51

18. South Stainley to Cayton and Markington.................... 54

19. Ripley to Ripon via Markington and Markenfield Hall 56

20. Ripon to Studley Park... 60

Where the walks start

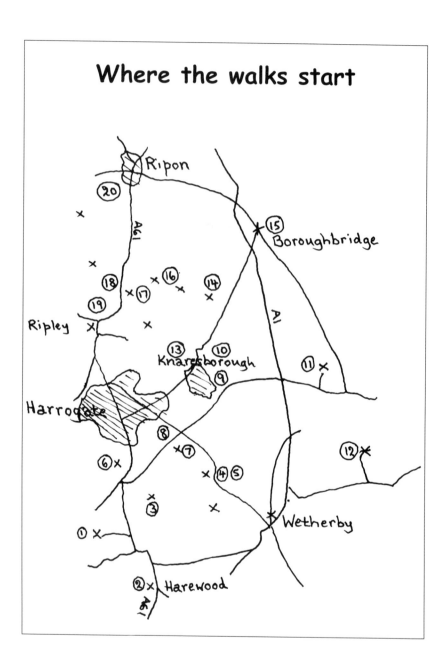

Introduction

Whether you live in Harrogate or are a visitor, you do not need to go far to find attractive walking country. There are many good walks on your doorstep! And in every direction!

This book describes twenty walks in the local countryside. It is a rolling landscape of low hills and shallow valleys cloaked in pastures and arable fields where the lower slopes of the Pennines merge into the Vale of York. From many points there are fine views over to the Pennines, and in the other direction across to the escarpment of the North York Moors (the Kilburn White Horse is often clearly visible). There is also plenty of parkland. One of the walks goes through the well-known Harewood Park and other enjoyable routes take walkers through Studley Park close to Fountains Abbey and Ribston Park near Knaresborough.

An unusual feature in the landscape is a narrow belt of magnesian limestone that runs north east from near Spofforth (it originates north of Nottingham and ends up in the cliffs north of Sunderland). Here, it is spectacularly seen in the riverside cliffs at Knaresborough, and the rock is also exposed in the Valley of the Bridges in Studley Park. The limestone is also to be seen at Lime Kiln Quarry (now a nature reserve) near Burton Leonard where it nourishes a distinctive flora.

This is a countryside where there is plentiful wildlife. The quiet walker will see roe deer and hares from time to time. Rabbits and pheasants are ubiquitous. There are not only hedgerow and woodland birds, but many waders, ducks and geese on the ponds and lakes. Skylarks are recovering in numbers and their cascade of song up above can often be heard. One of the walks goes beside the well-known ponds at Staveley, and several include attractive stretches of riverside walking beside the Nidd, Ure or Wharfe. Red kites may well be seen near Harewood, where they were re-introduced a few years ago, and they are spreading into the surrounding countryside (and have been seen in Harrogate!).

The walks visit many pleasant villages. These are now mainly commuter and retirement settlements, but the buildings from a previous age have generally been sensitively converted to modern use, and recent developments have been fairly small scale and blend well. Two villages of particular historical interest are Spofforth, where the castle, with more extensive ruins than they seem from the roadside, was once the home of the Percy family, before they moved to Northumberland, and Aldborough, once an important Roman town. There are also interesting small towns in the area: the attractions of Knaresborough and Ripon are well-known, but Boroughbridge should certainly not be overlooked and the Devil's Arrows at Boroughbridge are one of the most impressive "prehistoric" sites in the whole of England.

The walks in this volume are broadly to the east of Harrogate. They are east of a hypothetical fuzzy line a mile or two west of the A61. You gain a good idea of the local landscape if you take a seat on the upper deck of the No.36 bus as it goes along the A61 on its journey from Leeds to Harewood, Harrogate, Ripley and Ripon. You can use this valuable and comfortable bus service (every twenty minutes) to reach the start of several of the walks. Nearly all the other walks are accessible by public transport, but except to Knaresborough the services are less frequent.

The sketch maps accompanying the description of each walk are greatly simplified and are intended only as an overview of the route. They should not be relied on as an alternative to the walk description, and it is strongly recommended that the appropriate Ordnance Survey maps be bought. All of the walks are to be found on Explorer 289 Leeds, Harrogate, Wetherby and Pontefract, and 299 Ripon & Boroughbridge. These maps will not only help you to trace the walks described in this book, but will, it is hoped, suggest further walks for exploring the attractive local countryside.

The walks are between five to six miles in length on average, and are ideal for a half day walk, though in the summer months you may wish to linger. In summer they can all be done in trainers or a strong pair of shoes, but in the winter months soil often turns to mud and boots are essential. All the paths used are definitive rights of way or permissive footpaths or footpaths to which the public has traditionally not been denied access. At the time of writing there were no obstructions, though a number of the stiles were in poor repair and paths are not always reinstated after ploughing. If you encounter any obstructions (and this includes high crops across the path), nuisances or other difficulties, please report them to the Rights of Way Officer, North Yorkshire County Council, County Hall, Northallerton, DL7 8AD.

This book of walks has a companion volume *Country Walks Around Harrogate: Volume 2 West* in which twenty walks mainly in Nidderdale and the Washburn Valley are described. Both books are overdue replacements of *Popular Walks Around Harrogate* (ed. J. Dickinson 1991, S. Barclay 1998), and its predecessor *Walks Around Harrogate* (ed. P. Goldsmith, 1972, 1974) which are now out of print (a clear indication of their popularity).

An immense amount of useful work in protecting local rights of way and in making them more accessible by waymarking them and by building stiles and footbridges is done by the Harrogate Group of the Ramblers' Association, to whom all local walkers owe a debt of gratitude. We hope that all who use this book will consider becoming members of the Association, further details of which can be found on the opposite page.

Keith Wadd
Chairman, Ramblers' Association West Riding Area
December 2007

The **Ramblers' Association**, a registered charity, is an organisation dedicated to the preservation and care of the countryside and its network of footpaths, and to helping people to appreciate and enjoy them.

Through its National Office the Ramblers' Association lobbies and campaigns for more effective legislation to achieve

- the preservation and improvement of the footpath network
- better access to the countryside
- the preservation and enhancement for the benefit of the public of the beauty of the countryside.

Since its formation in 1935 the Ramblers' Association has grown into a powerful campaigning organisation, its latest success being the achievement of the Right to Roam on mountain, moorland, heath, down and common land in 2000.

The Association relies on many volunteers working at Area and Local Group level to help achieve these objectives.

The **West Riding Area** is one of the 51 Areas of the Ramblers' Association which cover England, Wales and Scotland. It includes the whole of West Yorkshire and parts of North Yorkshire around Selby, York, Harrogate, Ripon, Skipton and Settle, as well as the southern part of the Yorkshire Dales National Park. The Area has more than 4,000 members and is divided into 14 Local Groups.

The **Local Groups** (among them Harrogate and Ripon) carry out the work of the Ramblers' Association by keeping an eye on the state of footpaths in their area and monitoring proposed closures and diversions.

- They put pressure on their Local Authority to take action to remove obstructions and re-instate footpaths after ploughing.
- They do practical work of footpath clearance and waymarking, and can erect stiles and footbridges.
- Where the Local Authority has set up consultation procedures, e.g. Footpath and Access Forums, the Local Group will normally send a representative.
- Most Local Groups produce their own programme of walks.

Regular walks are a very important part of Ramblers' activities. As well as ensuring that local footpaths are used, they provide healthy recreation and the opportunity to make new friends. There are walks organised by the Harrogate Group every Saturday.

If you use and enjoy the footpath network, please help us to protect it, by joining the Ramblers' Association. For further information contact

The Ramblers' Association, 2nd Floor, Camelford House, 87-90 Albert Embankment, London SE1 7TW (Tel.: 020 7339 8500, Fax.: 020 7339 8501; e-mail: ramblers@ramblers.org.uk).

Or visit our websites: www.ramblers.org.uk, www.ramblersyorkshire.org.uk, www.willouby.demon.co.uk/ramblersassociation/harrogategroup.htm

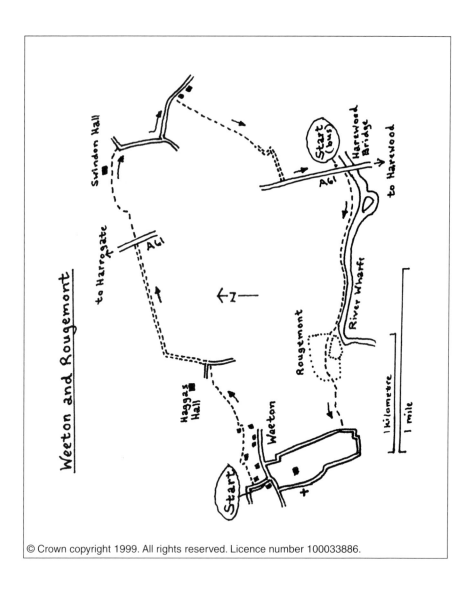

1. WEETON and ROUGEMONT

6¼ miles/10 km. Explorer 289 Leeds. Riverside and woodland, field paths and an old track. Fine views of Lower Wharfedale. After much rain one crossing of a beck may be impossible, but the problem can be circumvented by a mildly adventurous scramble.

Harrogate-Leeds bus to the stop before Harewood Bridge. Cross the road, turn left towards the bridge and start the walk at [*] below.
Park cars considerately in Weeton village, perhaps at the bottom of Weeton Lane, where it leaves Main Street.

Walk up Weeton Lane. Between the two last houses on the right cross a stile into an enclosed path, which leads to another stile into a field. Follow the left hand edge of the field to a fine old stile in the corner. Turn left along the track for a few yards and go through the first large gate on the right. Walk along the right hand edge of the next field to a stile in the corner, then keep forward between gardens. Bend slightly

"... a fine old stile in the corner"

right at the end to pass round a gate onto the end of a tarmac road. A few yards along this road take the fenced path on the left.

Pass through a small gate and walk straight forward, to pass through a small gate beside a large one into a house garden. Walk forward and turn sharp left at the end of the building on the left to walk along by a high fence on the left to another small gate. Go through and turn right to cross a footbridge. Head for the top left hand corner of the next large field, where you will find a stile. Cross and continue up the left hand edge of the next field, passing to the right of the bushes rather than going through them. At the top of the hill pause to look back at the view over Weeton and Lower Wharfedale.

Cross the stile in the corner and turn left up the tarmac lane, but in a few yards, when the tarmac bends left through the gateway of Haggas Hall, keep straight on up the track. At the top of the hill near a tall telephone mast the track turns sharp right. Follow it to the A61. Cross diagonally right, go through the bridle gate and bear slightly right down the field. At the bottom of the field go through the gate, cross the stone bridge over the beck, go through another gate and walk up the next field with the hedge on your right. Go through the gate in the corner and continue up the next field, now with the fence on your left.

When you reach the buildings of Swindon Hall Farm, bear right across the grass to a wall corner, walk past the imposing gateway into the Hall on your left, go through a gate and follow the hedge on your right down to join the farm access road. Follow this down to a motor road, which you reach on a bend. Ignore the road to the left and keep straight on. At the next road junction turn left (signposted Kearby). Kirkby Overblow is on the ridge over to the left. Immediately before the first house on the right go through the small gate beside the large double gate on the right and walk down the left hand edge of two fields.

Go through the gate into the third field and walk straight forward across it. Pass under power lines and pass close to a telegraph pole under more overhead wires. You should by now see a stile in the fence at the bottom of the field. It is in fact two stiles with a footbridge between them. Cross and bear half right on the track over the field. Having crossed the bridge into the next field, bear half left across it, leaving the track which follows the hedge. On the far side of the field you join another track: bear left along it, but in a few yards it turns right and crosses a ditch, soon to follow a hedge on the right back to the A61.

Cross the road and turn left along the narrow footway. [*] Immediately before Harewood Bridge turn right through a gate, and when you are faced by a closed gate in a wall, turn left through a kissing-gate and bear right along the river bank. After some time you will reach a stile in a fence. Cross and bear left down to the river bank again. Soon you will drop down some steps, cross a feeder beck and climb some steps up the other side. (This crossing may be impossible after heavy rain. In this case turn right parallel to the beck for a few yards, drop down the bank to it, it is quite narrow and can be crossed on stones, then scramble up the bank on the other side into the field and turn left along the field edge, where you will shortly rejoin the main route.)

Soon the clear path climbs steps away from the river into a field. Turn left along the field edge, which soon turns right away from the river. A short way along turn left into the woods. The path bears right, then left again and you reach a fork. Keep left, i.e. straight on, but take time to read the information panel erected by the Kirkby Overblow Local History Group in 2005.

You are close to the site of Rougemont Castle, "the remains of an ancient ringwork, a type of fortification which occurs from the late Anglo-Saxon period to the early Middle Ages, the administrative centre of the Manor of Harewood. It comprised a D-shaped fortified enclosure bounded by a bank and surrounding ditch. Masonry remains indicate that the bank was probably surmounted by a wall. The ringwork contained the residence of the Lord of the Manor, along with other domestic buildings. An outer bank and ditch, surrounding the ringwork to the west, north and east, enclosed the bailey, which would have contained garrison and utility buildings and pens for corralling stock and horses. The location of some of these features is indicated by the presence of platforms and earthworks. To the west of the site a marshy area reflects the remains of former fishponds to serve the manor. The site was abandoned c.1366, when Harewood Castle was built on a sloping spur of land to the south of the River Wharfe.

Follow the path to the far side of the wood, where a stile by a gate gives access to a field. Bear half left across the field to a small gate. Cross the stone packhorse bridge, go through another gate and walk straight across the next field to join a track. Follow this along past the sewage works, after which the track bends right. In a few yards go through the large double gate on the left and follow the track to a narrow tarmac road. You can either go left or right here. Going left is slightly longer

Packhorse bridge

and takes you past the church and old vicarage. If you choose to go left, when you reach the main road in the village, turn right and then left into Weeton Lane, if you choose to go right, when you reach the main road in the village, turn left and then right into Weeton Lane.

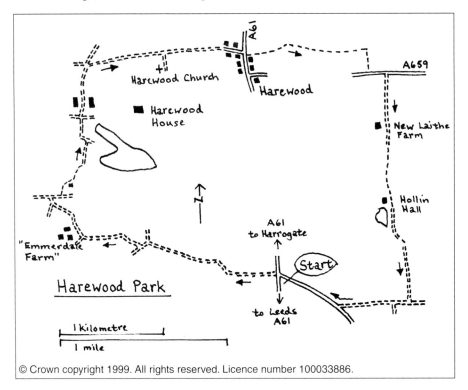

11

2. HAREWOOD PARK

6½ miles (10¼ km); Explorer 289 Leeds. An easy ramble almost entirely on tracks, partly through the parkland and woods of the Harewood Estate, with excellent views of Wharfedale.

Harrogate-Leeds bus to Wike Lane, about 1¼ miles beyond Harewood village on the A61 to Leeds. There is a large gate into Harewood Park and a former lodge. By car: Coming from Harrogate on the A61 to Leeds, drive for 1¼ miles past Harewood village and turn left into a minor road signposted to Wike. A few yards along this road there is a large layby with a memorial seat. Park here (GR 326 432) and return to and cross the main road.

Go through the right hand of the three large gates and head along the track through the park. Immediately there is a fine view right to Harewood House and Lower Wharfedale. *(Harewood House, one of Yorkshire's most beautiful stately homes, was designed by the York architect John Carr in the mid-18th century, and the interiors are by Robert Adam. It is open to visitors. The Park was designed by Capability Brown.)* Follow the track to another gate into a wood. Cross an 18th century stone bridge and bear left (bridleway sign). At the next fork keep right (signpost: you will note that you are on the Leeds Country Way). Shortly before you reach the end of the wood, fork right at a junction of tracks (signpost) and cross the shallow valley of Stub House Beck. The buildings over to the left are the set for YTV's "Emmerdale Farm". At the next crossing fork right on a descending track, soon coming to a T-junction where again you bear right downhill.

Harewood House and Park

The track leads to a gate into a field, but 200 yards before this, fork left onto another descending track, which leads to the left of a stone barn. Pass through the gate and keep forward down the track. The lake and the house are seen in the distance. Bear left at the next junction, and the track soon curves right to a gate. Pass to the left of an old walled garden. You are joined by a tarmac track from the right, and soon there is a fine view over Wharfedale to Weeton and Almscliff Crag. Drop to a crossroads: a short distance over the bridge on the right is Harewood House, but there is no right of way to it. Keep forward over another bridge then uphill through the Home Farm, now converted into offices.

Cross a cattle-grid to re-enter the park. Walk forward to a junction (another nice view, and deer can often be seen around here), where you bear right uphill. Cross another cattle-grid. *(The track on the right at this point leads to the 15th-century Harewood Parish Church, now in the care of the Churches Conservation Trust and open every afternoon in summer. The interior contains a spectacular and fascinating collection of alabaster tombs, dating from 1419 to 1510, commemorating the owners of Harewood and of a nearby estate, Gawthorpe.)* Our walk continues straight ahead to Harewood village. Keep forward to the main road, cross it (care!) and turn right, but only as far as the Harewood Arms.

Immediately before the pub take the signposted path on the left, a tarmac lane. At the gate into Maltkiln House the lane bears slightly right, and when the tarmac ends cross the stile by the gate ahead and keep forward along the track with a small wood to the right (another fine view left over Wharfedale). Cross the stile by the next gate and keep forward along the track (permissive bridleway). When you reach a signposted track on the right, turn along it and follow it to the A659 Harewood to Wetherby road.

Turn left along the road. Shortly after passing the long layby cross the road and take the farm access road opposite. When the road forks just before New Laithe Farm, keep left and pass round the left hand end of the farmhouse onto a concrete track, and when this ends keep straight forward downhill with a hedge to your right to another gate. Keep forward down the next large field to a gate near the left hand end of a row of tall trees. The gate is quickly followed by another one, and now you must bear slightly left uphill (no clear path) to the left hand end of the buildings of Hollin Hall ahead. Pass to the left of the house and walk straight downhill on a track to pass to the left of a lake. When you reach the wood bear right up to a gateway, then left on the track along the outside edge of the wood.

The track soon bears slightly right uphill away from the wood, and when it peters out keep forward to a gate in the top left hand corner of the field. Now there is a clear track again, up with the hedge to your left. Enter a hedged track and follow it up to a T-junction, where you turn right along the track. When it forks, keep right, i.e. straight on, soon passing to the left of Wike Wood. At the motor road turn right to return to the starting point.

3. CLAP GATE AND BARROWBY

4½ miles (7¼ km). Explorer 289 Leeds. Field paths, old bridleways, fine views over Wharfedale. The last section of bridleway can be very muddy after wet weather.

Park in Kirkby Overblow on the road opposite the Shoulder of Mutton. No public transport.

Near the bus stop there is an interesting information panel about the history of the village. From the road junction by the Star & Garter take the road towards Wetherby. At a small triangle of grass, *with trees planted to commemorate the coronation of King Edward VII in 1902*, fork left off the road along a track. Cross the cattle-grid and immediately fork right along the right hand edge of the field. At the end of the field keep to the left of the power line pole and walk down the right hand edge of the next field. In the next corner go through the large gate on the right and follow the path across a patch of rough ground to a stile.

Bear slightly right across the next field to a prominent wall corner and continue with the wall on your left. Cross a stile and continue along the left hand edge of the next field. When you reach the corner of the wood, kink left and cross the stile by the small gate into it and follow the path along the inside edge of the wood. Leave the wood through another gate and immediately turn right through a metal gate. Walk along the right hand edge of five fields (there is a very wet patch in the fourth one). At the end of the fifth field go through the gate on the right and turn left along an enclosed path.

Follow this pleasant hedged bridlepath to where it ends at a gate into a field. Go through and walk straight across the field on a broad grassy path. Cross a ditch and keep forward to a fence corner. Follow the fence on your left only for about 20 yards, then turn sharp right and walk across the middle of the field on a fairly clear path, following an old field boundary marked at first by a shallow dip on your right, then by a straggly hedge. Go through the gate ahead into a hedged track and follow it to a road.

Turn right to Clap Gate, where the house on the right used to be a pub. Bend right with the road, and a few yards after the last house cross a stile on the right and bear fairly sharply left over the field, passing just to the left of a power line pole, from where you will see the next stile ahead. Cross and bear very slightly right over the next field to reach the next stile, and slightly right again over the next field, aiming for the right hand of the three buildings on the far side. The middle building is Kearby Methodist Church. Cross the stile, walk through the small grass enclosure to a gap in the fence at the end and turn left up the track to the road, where there is a bench.

Cross the road and go through the gateway opposite. Fine views open up over Wharfedale. Keep straight on past the farm, but don't go through the gate and over the cattle-grid. Follow the grassy path down to another gate. The next part of the path is overgrown, so bear right into the field and walk down its left hand edge. Pass a barn, then cross the stile by a large wooden gate on the left and bear right down the farm access track. Follow it down to the road and turn right uphill to Barrowby. At the top there is another fine view over Wharfedale and to Almscliff Crag.

Barrowby is a charming spot. At the T-junction keep left, but in 100 yards turn right along Lund Head Lane. Having passed Lund Head Farm, keep forward for a short distance, then turn left up the hedged bridleway. A little further along don't go through the gate on the right into the field. The next section is well used by horses and can be muddy after a wet spell. After a time the path widens to a track which leads to a road. Turn right to return to Kirkby Overblow.

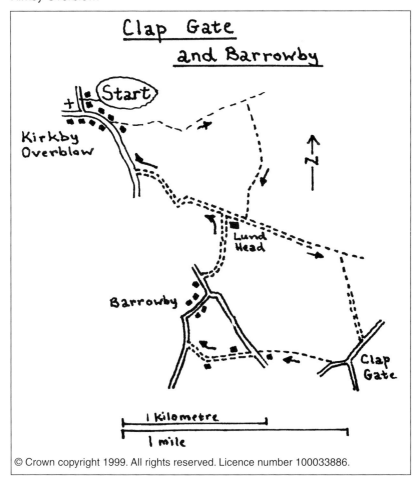

Clap Gate
and Barrowby

Start

Kirkby
Overblow

N

Lund
Head

Barrowby

Clap
Gate

1 Kilometre

1 mile

15

4. SPOFFORTH and SICKLINGHALL

4 miles/6½ km. Explorer 289 Leeds. Good tracks link two attractive villages.

770 bus Harrogate-Wetherby-Leeds to Spofforth. Alight at the stop just past the castle. Park on the main street near the castle towards the northern end of the village.

There is an interesting information panel here on the history of the village. Spofforth is mentioned in the Domesday-Book and one John Brabanner (a weaver from the Low Countries to judge by his name) was included in the Poll Tax return of 1379. The castle, the first English home of the Norman De Percy family, later Dukes of Northumberland, was forfeited to the Crown in 1407 after the Battle of Bramham Moor and was in use as a hunting lodge well into the 17th century. The ruins are much more extensive than they look from the road. In the churchyard is the grave of Blind Jack of Knaresborough, the famous road builder.

Leave the village by walking along the A661 towards Wetherby, passing the Railway Inn (site of the old level crossing on the Harrogate-Wetherby line) and continuing along the footway that rises above the road to the entrance of Spofforth Hall. Turn right across the cattle-grid and leave the drive as it bears down left towards the Hall by following the track straight across the field to the gate in the corner. Keep on the track. Shortly after it bends left, it forks: keep straight on here between a fence and a line of old trees.

Follow the track until you pass through a gateway and reach a T-junction with a much better track (Stockeld Lane). Turn right down this and follow it to Sicklinghall. Continue along the road through the village, passing the pond, and up to the Scott's Arms. Turn right and walk straight through the car-park to the stile on the right of the gate. Cross it and walk down the drive of Sicklinghall Park, passing to the right of the stable block at the bottom and going through the gate ahead. Bear slightly left to a stile by another gate.

Follow the fence on your right to a double stile into the next field and turn left along the fence. In the next corner turn right and follow the hedge along to a stile in it by a gate. Cross it and turn right along the track. When the track bends right towards Whin Lane Farm, go through the bridle gate ahead and turn right along the hedge. In the next corner turn left, and a short distance further on turn right again through the hedge into a fenced track. Spofforth church tower can be seen half left ahead.

At the T-junction turn left. Follow this track to another T-junction and turn right along the lane which leads back to Spofforth. At the main road turn left for the village centre.

5.   SPOFFORTH TO KIRKBY OVERBLOW

6¼ miles/10 km. Explorer 289 Leeds. Easy, almost level walking on field paths and good tracks through pleasant arable and pastoral countryside. Both Spofforth and Kirkby Overblow have attractive houses.

770 bus Harrogate-Wetherby-Leeds to Spofforth. Alight at the stop just past the castle. Park on the main street near the castle towards the northern end of the village.

There is an interesting information board here. Walk along the main street towards the centre of the village. If you wish to visit the church, turn left at the roundabout, otherwise keep straight on for about 300 yards and turn right along Park Lane.

Follow this lane/track, ignoring all tracks forking left or right, until you reach

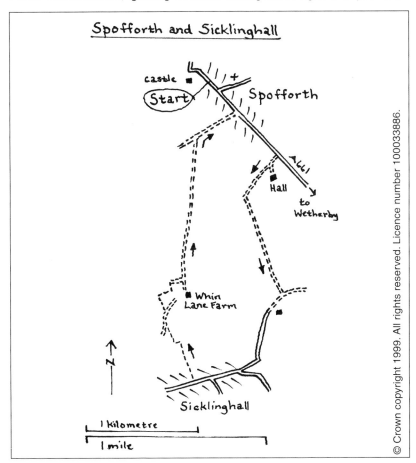

17

a track on the right signposted to Park House Farm (the name may be obscured, but it's a clear track leading to a complex of buildings). Ignore it too, but at the fork a little way further on keep right, i.e. straight on. At the end of a small wood on the left there may be a gate across the track by a disused cattle grid. Go through, and where the track turns sharp right to go to Parks Farm, walk forward into the field and keep along its left hand edge. When you reach a wood, the bridleway goes through the gate on the left, but we follow the footpath through the gate ahead into the wood.

Follow the left hand edge of the wood to another gate at the far end. Go left into the adjacent field, then keep your former direction with a wall on your right. Cross the stile ahead and keep on by the wall. When the wall turns sharp right, walk half right across the field to the stile in the wall opposite.

The path crosses rough ground to a large gate. Go through and turn left along the left hand edge of the field. When you reach a tarmac lane, turn left over the cattle grid, then right at the fork. Follow the road into the centre of Kirkby Overblow. Turn right at the junction by the Star and Garter. If you want to visit the church, take the lane on the left just after the pub, otherwise keep straight ahead.

There is an interesting information board by the bus shelter. Continue along the main street, passing Walton Head Lane on the left. Just after the school entrance on the left cross the road and cross the stile on the right. Walk down the field with a wood on the left. Cross the next stile and continue by the wall and then the fence on the left towards a red brick house. Cross

Kirkby Overblow church

the stile beside the gate ahead and walk down the tarmac drive, passing the house on your right, to a large gate ahead. Go through and walk down the next field to a gap in the hedge at the bottom. This is in fact a bridge over a beck. Cross and bear half left up towards a fence corner, then follow the fence on the right to the next stile.

Keep up the right hand edge of the next field. Cross the stile in the top corner and turn right along the edge of the next field, in a short distance turning left again with the hedge. When you come to a gap in this hedge, go through and continue your former direction, now with the hedge on your left. Cross a farm track and keep forward to a gate ahead in the corner of the field. Go through and bear half right across the next field, keeping well to the right of Sunrise Farm, to cross the farm track again by two stiles. Bear slightly left to a fence corner and keep the same direction across the rest of the field to a large gate in the fence ahead. Go through and turn left along the track.

At the T-junction with another track turn right. Pass through a gate beside a small wood and continue along the track. Where it forks, don't go through the gate ahead, but turn right. Where the track bends left again, you're joined by another one coming in from the right from Sunrise Lakes. Some distance further along another track comes in from the right. Shortly before the track bears left towards a wood, take the minor track forking right off it,

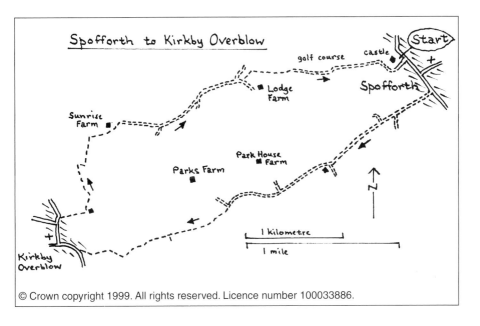

which soon leads to the access track to Lodge Farm. Cross this to the gate opposite (bridleway sign) and walk along the left hand edge of the field with Lodge Wood to your left.

Go through a gate and continue by the wood. At the end of the wood a track comes down from the farm on your right. Ignore this and fork left down through the gorse bushes to a bridle gate in the bottom corner. Cross the footbridge and bear right along the path. Spofforth golf course is on your left and after a while on the right too. The bridleway eventually bends right, passes through a narrow gateway ahead and bends left under the old railway viaduct. Spofforth Castle is now to your left. Join a gravel drive which becomes a tarmac street. Follow this back to the main road and the start of the walk.

6. PANNAL TO KIRKBY OVERBLOW

6¼ miles/10 km. Explorer 289 Leeds. Field paths, good views. There are several main roads to cross and the railway is crossed twice.

The car-park adjacent to Pannal Church is private, but cars can be parked in the road opposite, Crimple Meadows. Train to Pannal Station.

From Crimple Meadows turn right along Main Street, cross the bridge over the Crimple and turn right along Mill Lane. From the station walk down the road towards the village centre and turn left along Mill Lane. Look out for a footpath sign pointing right to Burn Bridge. Pass a pond on the left and bear left along beside it. Soon the Crimple is close by on the right. The path bears left across a wooden footbridge to follow a fence on the left. At the next collection of houses ignore the road on the right down to a bridge; keep forward, and a yard or two after four garages on the right turn left and then left again before the cricket ground for a yard or two to a stile, then bear half right to follow the fence on the left to a stile/footbridge, then continue up the left hand edge of the next field.

Cross the railway (care!) and keep on up the left hand edge of two fields to a gate and the A61. Cross the road (EXTREME CARE! Cars come round the blind bend on the right fast.) and turn right along to the corner. Don't go through the entrance gate, but cross the stile on the right immediately before it and turn left to follow the wall/fence on the left. Where this bends left, fork half right across the field to a stile in the fence. Cross the stile/footbridge/stile, then walk up the left hand edge of the field.

Cross the stile in the top corner, walk forward a few yards to cross another stile, then go half right over the next field to a stile and the A658. Cross to the stile opposite (care!) and follow the right hand edge of two fields, then a few yards of enclosed track, go through the left hand gateway ahead, then continue with the hedge/fence on your right. Turn left along the boundary wall of the farm, then right at the next corner. Look out for a stile in the hedge on the right, cross the grass to the stile opposite, just outside the gate of Walton Head House, and turn left along the drive to the road.

Cross to the stile opposite, then walk over the narrow field to the next stile and follow the left hand edge of two fields, crossing a stile between them. Cross the stile in the next corner and turn left with the field boundary. It's more or less a straight line from here to Kirkby Overblow. So keep along the left hand edge of the fields until a stile lands you in a field quite a distance from the left hand edge. Walk straight across the middle to a small metal gate, and now you will follow the right hand boundary of several fields, climbing first onto the ridge on which the village is built. Don't be tempted down the slope on the right. Eventually you reach a stile from which Kirkby Overblow church can be seen ahead. *The large white house on the right was built in 1931 "quite a historic monument now, in that it is among the early houses in England to adopt the new style of France and Germany"*

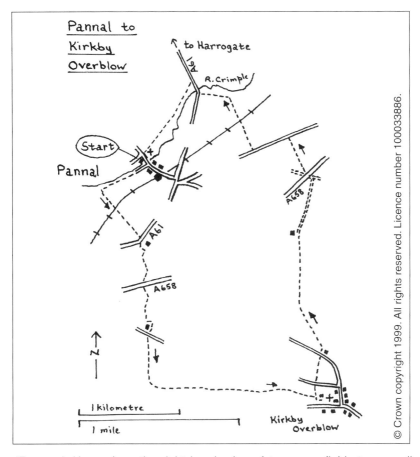

(Pevsner). Keep along the right hand edge of two more fields to a small metal gate.

The walk continues by turning left up the fenced path, but to visit the village cross the stile on the right, walk down between the hedge and the fence, cross the gravel drive diagonally left to another stile, bear slightly left to the gated stile in the corner and walk straight ahead into the churchyard. *The church has a few mediaeval features, but the nave is mostly of 1780 and the church was 'improved' in 1872 (Pevsner).* Walk past the church, through the gate and straight forward to reach the village centre with its two pubs. *There is an interesting information panel by the bus shelter, where one can learn that 'Overblow' first appears in the 13th century and probably means 'ore blowers', evidence of an iron smelting industry.*

To continue the walk return through the churchyard and up to the stile leading into the fenced path. Follow this to a tarmac lane, turn right and in

40 yards go left through a gate into another enclosed path. At the end go through another gate, cross the road diagonally right to the stile opposite and follow the right hand edge of the field uphill. Cross the stile in the corner and continue by the hedge on the right to the next stile. Cross the lane into the narrow fenced path opposite. At one point the path makes a sharp turn left then bends round to a stile.

Walk down the left hand edge of the next field. Cross a footbridge, go through a gate and keep on along the left hand edge of the next two fields. Go through a gate, and now the hedge is on the right. Go through a heavy metal gate and continue with the hedge/fence on your right towards the farm. Pass through the larger of the two gates at the end of this field into the farmyard and walk straight forward on the clear track between the buildings. On leaving the farm the track runs between hedges. Go through a gate and at the T-junction turn left up the tarmac lane to the A658.

Cross straight over (care!), go through the gate opposite, and ignoring the attractive tarmac lane ahead (Follifoot Lane) go through the gate on the right and follow the left hand edge of the field. Pannal golf course can be seen through the trees on the left. Pass through a gate and keep straight on. In a few yards the path broadens to a track. At the next road cross and turn left along the footway, in a few yards ignoring a bridleway sign on the right. Further on ignore another bridleway sign pointing into the wood. At the end of the wood a pleasant view opens up towards Harrogate.

At the end of the first field after the wood a footpath sign points right through two large gates. Walk down the left hand edge of the field and follow the track as it kinks left and right into the adjacent field. Now the hedge is on your right. Cross the railway line (care!) and continue along the right hand edge of two fields. Cross the stile and turn left along a rather rough path. Cross a small footbridge and follow the path to a stony track. Walk along this the short distance to its end and bear left up the bank to a gate and the A61.

Cross this busy road with great care and turn right along the footway. About 100 yards beyond the bridge over the Crimple turn left down the signposted track and go through the kissing-gate ahead, ignoring the stile on the left. A clear path leads over the field. This is not on the exact line of the right of way, which heads for a gap in the hedge 20 yards from the far left hand corner of the field, but it is in general use. Go through the facing hedge and bear slightly left to a gate on the far side of the field. Cross the ditch by the slab bridge, go through the next gate and follow the clear path across the middle of the next field towards the houses. Cross the stile and follow the track forward to join a stony track. A few yards along this cross the stile on the left into the churchyard. The path passes to the right of the church to reach the start of the walk. *By the bench outside the church car-park there is an interesting information board about Pannal.* To return to the station turn left along the road.

River Crimple at Spofforth

7. FOLLIFOOT and CRIMPLE BECK

4½ miles (7 km). Explorer 289 Leeds. Two attractive villages, castle, field paths and riverside. The name Follifoot is thought to derive from the Norse meaning 'place of the horse fight', a sport popular with the Vikings. The Saxon cross dates from the 7th or 8th century.

Park in the main street of Follifoot opposite the Harewood Arms. 770 Harrogate-Wetherby-Leeds bus to Follifoot (half-hourly, hourly on Sundays).

Walk up to the road junction at the top of the main street by the village cross and the imposing entrance into Rudding Park and turn right along the road to Knaresborough (Plompton Road). Pass the church and the former pinfold and follow the road out of the village. Having crossed the bridge over the River Crimple, turn right, cross the stile into the field and take the path parallel to the river. You are now going to follow the river all the way to Spofforth, so always keep to the path nearest to it. After a time notice the outcrops of millstone grit over on the slope to the left.

Follifoot Cross

As you approach a house ahead, look out for a footbridge over the river. Cross it and follow the fenced path to the Old Corn Mill. Cross a little stone bridge over the mill goit and keep along the walled path to the access drive to the mill. Walk along this, at the road junction keep straight on, and a short distance further at the crossroads again keep straight on up Beech Lane. This leads to the main road in Spofforth opposite the castle.

The castle entrance is to the right, the walk continues to the left. *At the end of the field on the right there is an information board with notes on the history of Spofforth.* Take the next street on the right, Manor Garth. When the tarmac ends, keep on along the stony drive. The path bends left and then right, to pass under the old railway viaduct. Pass through a gateway and keep forward along the bridleway. Soon you have Spofforth golf course on both sides. Ignore all tracks leading onto it. After a time there is a beck to your left, which you cross by a footbridge. Go through the gate and bear right up the slope between the gorse bushes.

Walk along with Lodge Wood on your right through this field and the next. Lodge Farm is over to your left. Another gate leads out onto the Lodge

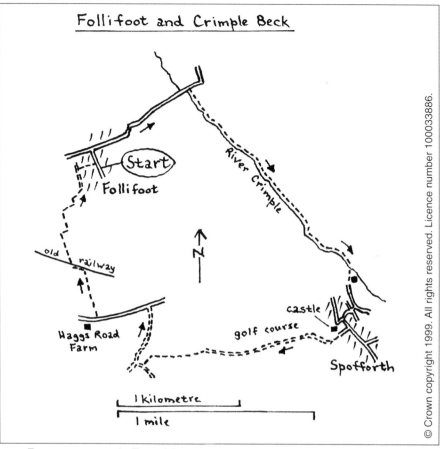

Follifoot and Crimple Beck

Start
Follifoot
River Crimple
old railway
Haggs Road Farm
N ↑
castle
golf course
Spofforth

1 kilometre
1 mile

Farm access track. Turn right down this, soon joining a metalled track: turn right along this and follow it up to Haggs Road. Turn left. Just as you reach the first buildings of Haggs Road Farm on the left, cross the stile by the gate on the right and walk down the right hand edge of the field, soon with a wood on your right. Follow the wood until you cross a stile and go down some steps onto the line of a former railway. Turn left along it for a few yards, then fork right off it again up to a field. Walk along its left hand edge.

Follifoot appears half right ahead. At the end of the field follow the boundary to the right, but go through a large gap on the left – there is a bench here – and walk down the left hand edge of the next field. Again turn right at the bottom. The path soon bears left out of the field and becomes hedged. When faced by large gates to the right and ahead, turn left. The path becomes a track. When the track turns right at Oakfield House, cross the step-stile ahead and walk along the enclosed path. This turns left, then left again, and now look out for a path junction where you must turn right, still in an enclosed path, down to the main street in Follifoot.

8. RUDDING PARK and the CRIMPLE VALLEY

7 miles/11¼ km. Explorer 289 Leeds. A most attractive round on field paths and good tracks through pleasant countryside with fine views.

The walk can be started at Hornbeam Park Station, where the large car-park is likely to be full on weekdays, but parking is available in nearby Beechwood Grove or on Hookstone Road beside the recreation ground; or in Follifoot, reachable by the Harrogate-Wetherby-Leeds bus and where there is parking in the Main Street near the Harewood Arms.

From the station walk along Hookstone Road in the direction of the Leeds-Harrogate road (A61), but take the bridleway on the left between houses 50 and 48 (signposted Leeds Road). When you are faced by the gate into the allotments, kink left, now on a tarmac path, and when the tarmac ends at a cross track, with a recreation ground to the left, keep forward along the track. When you reach a tarmac drive at the end, turn left.

[*] When the tarmac drive bends right through the gate into Longlands, keep straight forward along the track. Cross the railway bridge – the large viaduct is now over to the right – and pass round a gate to reach a road at the entrance to St. Michael's Hospice. Turn left for a short distance, then right through a wide entrance and walk along the access drive. In a short distance at the fork keep left on a narrower path. On reaching woodland at a junction, leave the track, which goes left to a gate, and keep straight forward over a stile by another gate. The path bends right and keeps along the edge of the wood, dropping gradually to the River Crimple.

Turn left over a footbridge over Hookstone Beck and follow the path along parallel to the river. Enter a field and join a concrete track and follow it along to a gate (the right of way actually follows the river, but you then need to pass through this gate). There is another massive viaduct to your right. Pass round the gate and continue along the concrete track, but in a short distance fork right off it along a signposted path which passes under the viaduct. At the top of the slope the path forks: keep left on a fairly level path through the wood, which comes to a step-stile by a gate into a field.

Walk straight across the middle of the field, halfway across bearing right to another stile by a gate. Walk forward up the path to another stile by a gate, then on along a better track. The Great Yorkshire Showground is over the hedge on the left. Pass to the right of the Traveller's Rest and follow the access road to a T-junction. Turn right downhill (no footway), cross the Crimple and follow the road up the other side.

At the top of the hill, where the road bends right, cross the stile in the wall corner on the left and walk along beside the Rudding Park wall. Cross the access road to Rudding Dower to another stile and continue by the wall. Rudding Park golf course is to your left. Cross a track passing through the wall and continue forward, now on another track, still with the wall to your

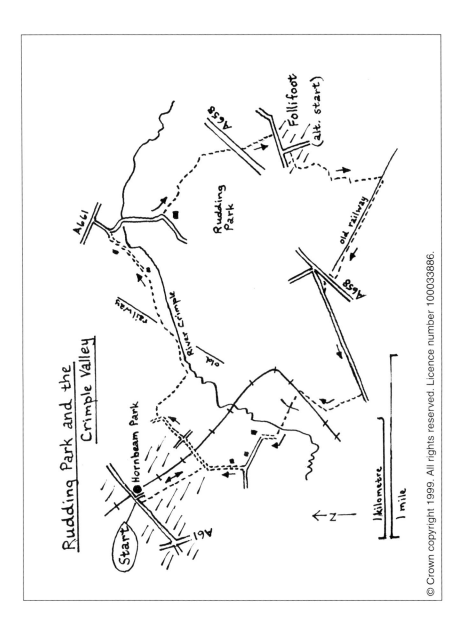

Rudding Park and the Crimple Valley

right. After a time keep with the wall when it turns right. When the track goes through a large double gate, fork left off it up by the wall to a stile and the A658, here the Harrogate southern bypass, which slices through Rudding Park.

Cross the road with great care to the stile opposite and walk up the left hand edge of the next field. Cross the next stile and walk up the edge of Follifoot churchyard to the next stile and turn right along the road through the village.

At the road junction by the Cross fork left, noticing the fine entrance to Rudding Park on the right. Cross the stile on the right opposite the Harewood Arms into an enclosed path (signposted Spofforth Haggs). At the end turn left, soon

Follifoot Cross and entrance to Rudding Park

right again and soon right again. The path ends at a stile: cross and bear right along the track. At the end of the houses follow the grassy path left, and when you are faced with a metal gate turn right. The path leads into a field: keep along the bottom edge, turning left with the path in the field corner.

Follow the path up to the next corner, where there is a seat, walk forward into the next field and turn right along the track. In the next corner turn left again and in the next one go through the kissing-gate on the right, drop to the track-bed of the old railway and bear right along it. After a time the track rises a little to a junction: keep straight on. When you reach a gate across the track, go through the kissing-gate beside it and keep forward along the next track. When faced by a gate and the A658 turn right, shortly turning left to pass through a tunnel under the main road.

Follow the track straight up the other side, go through a gate and emerge on a road. Cross to the footway and turn left. After a time the road climbs Follifoot Ridge and passes the entrance to Follifoot Hall. Continue to the start of the wood and take the signposted bridleway on the right. When the track is barred by a gate, the bridleway bears left into the wood. It is popular with riders and can be muddy. When you reach a T-junction, turn right and walk down close to the right hand boundary of the wood. In the bottom corner go through the gate into the field and turn right with a wall and a wood on your right.

At the end of the field continue along the enclosed track, soon turning left to cross a bridge over the Leeds-Harrogate railway. Walk straight down over the next field. Cross straight over the disused railway line at the bottom and continue down the right hand edge of the next field. At the bottom bear left and right with the fence, cross the River Crimple and walk up the right hand edge of the next field. The huge railway viaduct over the Crimple valley is over to your right. At the top of the field bear right, go through the gate and turn left up the tarmac lane.

When the lane bends left at the top of the hill, fork right off it along the access drive to Beech House and Longlands. When the road bends right, fork left off it along the track which leads back to Hornbeam Park Station. If you started the walk at Follifoot, ignore this track and jump to [*] above.

Knaresborough

29

9. KNARESBOROUGH, PLOMPTON, RIBSTON and GOLDSBOROUGH

9 miles/14½ km. Explorer 289 Leeds. Good tracks and footpaths through pleasant countryside and woodland, with two big houses and parkland.

Start in Knaresborough Market Square. From the train station walk up Kirkgate. From the bus station walk along High Street and left along Silver Street. Note that short stay car-parks in the town centre are limited to four hours.

Leave the Market Square where it narrows towards the Market Tavern and Castlegate, by turning left along Chapel Street. Follow it to its end and turn right downhill to Low Bridge. Cross the bridge, passing the Mother Shipton Inn, and part way up the hill turn left along Spitalcroft, a narrow tarmac lane. At the end continue along the footpath into the woods, climb until you are high above the river and reach a path junction. Turn left here, and keep left again immediately at the next fork on a descending path. At the bottom you follow a fence on the left and pass a house.

Keep forward a short way along the access drive, then straight on along a fenced path. At the end of the fenced section you enter another wood: a few yards along, fork right on an ascending path. It leads you to the top of the wood, where you bear left to reach a kissing-gate into the field on the right. Bear half left across this field, and soon you will see another kissing-gate. Go through this double one and keep forward up the slope, heading left of a group of four tall trees. Here you will reach a fence corner. Walk along with the fence on your right to a stile into Birkham Wood.

Walk forward for a few yards to join a better path and bear right along it. When the bridleway forks, keep straight ahead to cross the Harrogate southern bypass (care!) and take the bridleway opposite along the edge of a wood. After a time the path turns sharp right and joins a track: bear right along this. At the end of the field follow the track as it bends left. You are walking parallel to a hedge a few yards to your right. The path has been diverted round Plompton Hall, so at the end of this hedge turn right, pass the end of the hedge and walk down a track with a wood on the left.

At the end of the wood turn left, in a few yards turn right with the fence and go through a gate on the left at the bottom of the field. Follow the path across the middle of the field and leave it through a gate in the far left hand corner. Walk up the slope for a few yards, then turn right on a path through bushes, which leads to a bridle-gate. *Plompton Hall is to the left. Pevsner has this to say: "The Beauties of England and Wales say that Daniel Lascelles bought the estate in 1760, started to build a large mansion, but left it unfinished and later built 'an elegant little lodge' for himself. It looks as if that referred to the conversion of the centre of an ambitious stable block into living quarters".*

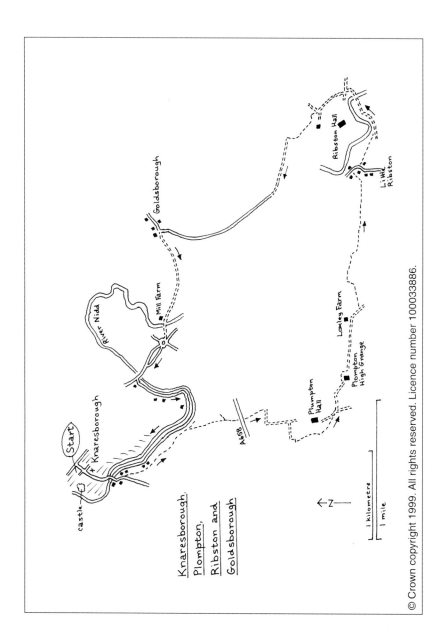

Knaresborough,
Plompton,
Ribston and
Goldsborough

31

Continue along the path to another bridle gate in the fence on the left and turn right along the tarmac road, immediately keeping left at the fork. Follow this road to Plompton Grange. Go through the entrance gateway and walk along the access drive between high hedges. Do not enter the gates beside the house, but fork left, still along the hedge, over a grassy patch through trees into a field and turn right along its edge. Cross the concrete to the left of a tall building, turn right at its end, then left at the T-junction. Follow this concrete road to Loxley Farm.

As you approach the farm, take the track forking right; pass to the right of the house and follow the track into the wood. Leave the wood and follow the track to where it bends right at another corner of the wood. Here fork left off the track to follow a hedge on the right. The field edge bends slightly left. Where it bends more sharply left, fork right into the corner, go through into the next field and turn right along the hedge on the right. Go through at the field corner into the next field, crossing a small plank bridge, and turn right round the field edge, turning left in the field corner.

Go through into the next field and keep on by the edge, which soon turns sharp right and then sharp left again. In a yard or two go through a gap in the hedge on the right and turn left, now with the hedge on your left. Follow this hedge to Little Ribston. As you approach the village, with overhead wires immediately ahead, the field boundary turns right: turn left at this point into the next field and follow the hedge on the right. Go through into the next field and in a few yards go through the gate on the right. Turn left, to pass to the left of a barn, at the end of which you turn right and walk down the field to a large gate out onto the road in the village.

Cross the road and turn right along the footway. In a short distance, where the road bends right, and just before a bus stop, turn left along a tarmac drive. Go through a gate and keep forward for 20 yards, then turn right into the garden of a house. Walk past the end of the house to a gate into Ribston Park and bear half left over the grass. Eventually you will reach a stile in a fence. Cross and keep the same line to the fence on the left, with the River Nidd beyond, and follow the fence to a concrete access road. Turn left along it.

Cross the river by a stone bridge. At the crossroads keep straight on. *To the left is the late 17th-century Ribston Hall with a*

The path crosses the 18th Century bridge in Ribston Park

32

mediaeval chapel adjoining it. Continue along the concrete road until you reach a fork: both branches lead to houses, but you leave the road here and keep straight on with the fence on your left. Go through the first gate you come to in this fence, and continue with another fence on the left. Bend right at the top of the slope, cross a stile by a gate ahead and continue by the fence on the left.

A stile by a gate ahead gives access to a wood: follow the track through the wood and leave it over a stile by another gate. Keep forward along the left hand edge of the field. Go through a gate, cross a stream by a stone bridge and continue along the left hand edge of the next field. Reach a tarmac road and keep forward along it to Goldsborough. At a junction on the edge of the village, turn left along a track with the duckpond on your left. Follow this track to Goldsborough Mill Farm, walk through the yard, cross the Nidd by the bridge and walk up to the main road, ignoring a track forking left halfway up.

Cross the road and turn right along the footway. Cross the bypass with the roundabout on your right, bear right along the footway, but in a few yards fork left on a tarmac path, then continue down the following road. When you reach the main road, bear left down the footway, cross the Nidd once more by Grimbald Bridge and turn left along Abbey Road.

This road is an attractive and interesting way back to the town centre. *A short distance along on the left are the steps which lead down to St. Robert's Cave. Several of the houses along here have the word 'abbey' or 'priory' in their names: there never was an abbey, but there was the mediaeval priory of St. Robert, of which nothing now survives except for a few stone fragments incorporated into a garden wall and the end of an outbuilding (at a house called The Priory). Much further along is the Chapel of Our Lady of the Crag, carved in the cliff, with the huge figure of St. Robert in full armour.*

When you reach Low Bridge, either turn right and walk uphill to the town centre or continue along Waterside to reach steps to the castle and the town centre.

10. HAY-A-PARK and CONEYTHORPE

7 miles/11½ km. Explorer 289 Leeds. Field paths and tracks through the pleasant countryside east of Knaresborough. Best done in a dry period, as much of the outward route can be wet and muddy after rain.

The walk starts in the Market Square in Knaresborough. From the train station walk up Kirkgate, from the bus station walk along High Street and left along Silver Street. Town centre car-parks, but note that short stay car-parks in the town centre are limited to four hours.

Leave the Market Square by the narrow Silver Street, which passes the Hart Inn. At the end keep forward past the bus station along the main road, cross left at the traffic lights and walk down Park Row. Bend left with the road and follow it downhill, crossing it when convenient. Notice the old horse troughs on the way down. When the road bends left again, turn right down Stockwell Lane, crossing it at the pedestrian crossing by the school. Turn left along Hambleton Grove. At the end of the terrace of houses on the right ignore the gap in the barrier into playing fields and turn right down the fenced footpath.

Cross the railway, go through the gate and continue with the fence on your right. At the next path junction turn right along a stretch of former railway line. Pass to the left of commercial buildings, with grass on your left, at the T-junction cross the road and turn right, but turn left along the first street. Enter the new housing development and in a few yards bear left at the T-junction. Don't turn right into Sterling Chase, but keep straight on along an asphalt path with a high hedge to the right. Cross the stile at the far end into a large field and turn left to follow the field boundary to a stile in the far left hand corner. Turn right along the lane for a short distance to a stile on the left.

Follow the right hand edge of the field, at first with a small wood on the right. At the end of the wood keep straight forward across the middle of the large field, aiming to the right of a house in the distance. On the far side cross a stile by a gate – there is a large lake down on the right – and follow the path forward over rough ground, then through light woodland, to climb to a stile onto a track. Bear right along this, soon between hedges. Look out for a large gate on the right with a blue bridleway waymark on it: go through and follow the track across the field.

Follow the track, well used by horses, all the way to Hopewell House Farm. Pass to the left of most of the buildings, then fork left up the continuation of the track. Very soon ignore a minor track forking left and shortly afterwards at a fork with an old stone gatepost between the branches keep left. Look out for another minor track forking left with a waymark and map which indicates the start of a new permissive bridleway, but don't take it. Eventually you pass an isolated brick building on the left and the track bends right and then left and heads for The Hollies Farm.

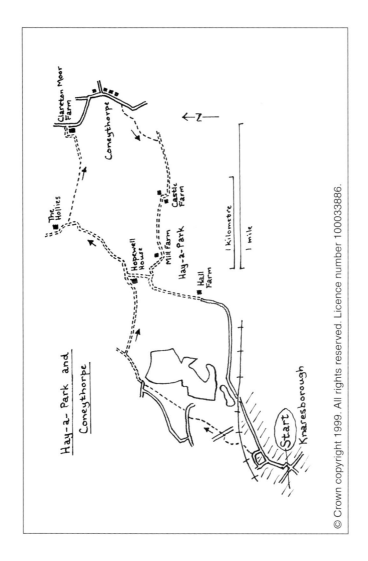

Hay-a- Park and Coneythorpe

Clareton Moor Farm
Coneythorpe
The Hollies
Hopewell House
Mill Farm
Castle Farm
Hay-a-Park
Hall Farm
Knaresborough
Start

←N—

1 Kilometre
1 mile

35

A few yards after this bend turn right off the track at a Knaresborough Round sign and follow the right hand edge of a field. In the next corner ignore the gap ahead and turn right through another gap, then bear half left over the next field. Go through a gap in the next hedge keep the same line across the next field until you hit a track. Bear left along this, under overhead wires and with a hedge on the right. At Clareton Moor Farm the track bends left and then right round the outside of the buildings to a road.

Turn right along the road and follow it to Coneythorpe. Walk through the village, passing the Tiger Inn. A short distance after leaving the village a track on the right is signposted as a public footpath. Follow this, but immediately after crossing a ditch turn left and walk along with the ditch on your left. When you reach a facing hedge, you want to go through it: there is a gap a few yards to the right. Now pay careful attention to route finding. A path should be visible leading through the crop to the hedge on the far side. If it isn't, look across to the far side and you will see that to the left of a good, solid stretch of hedge there is a section of rather more straggly hedge. Head for the join between the two sections (aiming well to the left of the Knaresborough church spire in the distance), and you will see that there is a marker post with a yellow arrow indicating a gap in the hedge. It is essential to find this. Go through and follow a fence on your right in the next field, but where this turns right, keep straight across the middle of the next field (again the path should be visible) to reach a farm access road. Turn right along it.

Interestingly the deep ditch that the track crosses is called on the map The Rampart, marking a line of ancient fortification, and the next farm is Castle Farm, the farmhouse being built on a mound. When you reach the farm, turn sharp right with the track between the buildings, then sharp left again, but when the track turns right again out of the farm, keep straight ahead through a wooden gate, then follow the left hand edge of the field on the raised track. Pass through a gate and continue along the track, which soon acquires a hard surface. The track bends right through Mill Farm, after which it is tarmac. At the T-junction turn left – over to the right is the imposing Hopewell House, round the back of which you passed earlier. When the road forks just before Hall Farm, take either branch.

After a time you pass the grounds of Knaresborough Rugby Club and soon under the Harrogate-York railway line. Pass The Forest School and at the crossroads keep straight on along Stockwell Lane. After a time you pass Hambleton Grove, which you went along earlier. Now follow your outward route back to the start.

11. WHIXLEY and ALLERTON MAULEVERER

5¼ miles (8½ km). Explorer 289 Leeds. Good tracks and field paths through flat, but attractive countryside. Two interesting churches.

Coming from Harrogate on the A59, some way after crossing the A1 take the minor road on the left signposted Whixley 1 mile. On reaching the village, the main road bends right (Stone Gate), but keep straight on (Clockhill Field Lane) and park by the wall on the left just before the road junction with West Lane and Church Street.

Start the walk by walking back along Clockhill Field Lane and out of the village. Pass Braker Lane on the right, and after a bend or two look out for a footpath sign on the left pointing right through a gap in the hedge. Walk along the right hand edge of two fields, then straight over the middle of the next one – there may be a grass headland – to a gateway on the far side (you may need to go a few yards left to reach it), then continue with the hedge on the right. Follow the field edge up to the brow of the hill and down the other side, drop into the next field and keep along its right hand edge. Rainshaw Farm is a field's length away to your left.

The footpath actually bears left away from the field edge to a stile in the hedge in front, but at the time of writing a temporary diversion keeps you along the edge, so you have to turn left at the far end to reach the stile. Cross it and bear very slightly right across the next field, parallel to the fence/hedge on your right (no path) to a large gate in the fence ahead. Go through and bear half left over the next large field towards a straggly line of trees: keep this on your right to reach a stile in the hedge onto the A59.

Turn right along this busy road and cross to the large parking layby opposite. Near the far end of this, perhaps obscured by a refreshment van, there is a stile in the hedge. Cross it and walk straight over the small rough field to the hedge opposite and turn right to cross a footbridge. Follow the left hand edge of the next field for a few yards to a stile on the left, cross and turn right along the field edge, but after a short distance bear slightly left away from it and head for a large solitary tree in the far hedge. To the right of the tree there is a stile: cross and keep the same direction over the next field to a track and a gate in the far left corner. Follow the track out onto the road in Hopperton and turn right along it.

From now on route finding is easy. Pass the Mason's Arms and follow the lane to the A59. Turn left along the footway, but after a few yards cross the road to the footway opposite. This leads through an archway in a hedge. Pass to the left of the cottage and turn right along the road to Allerton. Already the church at Allerton Mauleverer is visible. Pass the entrance on the left to Allerton Park Caravan Park, and when the road forks, keep right.

The church of St. Martin, now looked after by the Churches Conservation Trust and always open, is a curious building largely dating from 1745 but with 'Norman' features. Inside, the south arcade dates from the 14th

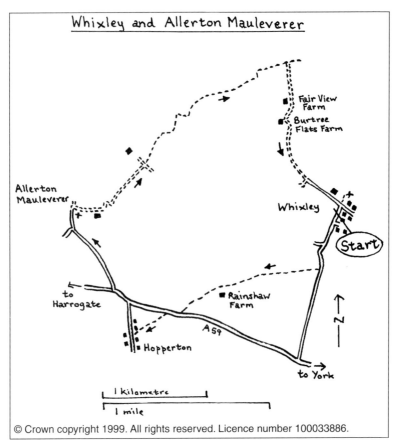

century and there is a fine hammer-beam roof. The large, mainly Victorian Allerton Park (or Castle) is to the left over the road.

Immediately after the church turn right along the farm access road. Walk straight through the farm and continue along the lane. When you reach a cross track, with a house some way to the left, keep forward on grass with a wood on the right. In the corner the path bears right through the wood. On emerging from the wood, keep forward with the hedge on your left. In the next corner cross through the field boundary ahead and turn right, now following the hedge on your right. In the next corner turn left with the hedge. About halfway along the field there is a signpost on the right: turn right past the signpost, then immediately left again, following the direction of Little Ouseburn, not Whixley (that would be a short cut back to Whixley).

You are now on Ox Close Lane. Ox Close Farm is over to the right. At the end of the first field you pass into an old path between hedges. At the end

of the hedged section the path kinks left and then right again and in a few
yards is again between hedges. At the end of this section again go left for a
few yards, then right again – Kilburn White Horse is visible over to the left –
continuing with the hedge on the right. At the end of this field there is
another signpost, and this time we do head for Whixley. So turn right and
follow the track with the hedge on your left.

Pass Fair View Farm, after which the surface is tarmac. A short distance
further on you pass through Burtree Flats Farm. Now follow the lane back to
Whixley. When you reach the village you pass the fine Whixley Hall on the
left, and just before the road junction a path on the left leads up to the early
14th century church. Your car should be waiting at the junction.

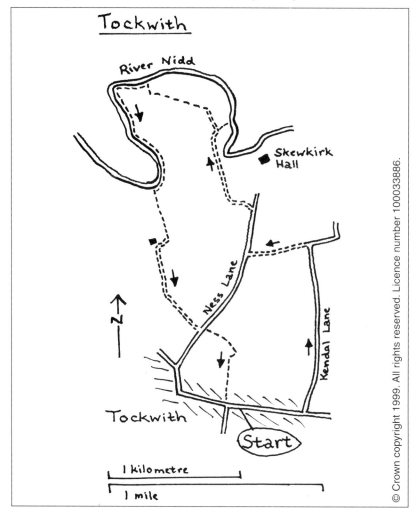

39

12. TOCKWITH RIVERSIDE

4½ miles (7¼ km). Explorer 289 Leeds. An easy stroll through the flat arable countryside in the Vale of York, mainly on tracks and clear field paths and including a pleasant stretch by the River Nidd.

On-street parking near the road junction in the centre of Tockwith. Bus 412/413 Wetherby-York (Mon-Sat hourly).

From the road junction walk along the main road (Marston Road) in the direction of York. Pass a children's playground on the left and about 300 yards further on turn left along Kendal Lane. Follow this lane/metalled track until it turns sharp right. At this point turn left through a bridle gate and follow a broad hedged way (this is Moor Lane across Tockwith Moor) to a tarmac lane (Ness Lane). Turn right along it.

At the entrance to Skewkirk Hall turn left along a hedged track. *After some distance, where the track turns left, if you were to go straight ahead through the bridle-gate you would reach the site of Skewkirk Bridge over the Nidd, which linked Tockwith to Kirk Hammerton. It existed for centuries before being demolished in 1969. Several groups including the Ramblers' Association have been campaigning long and hard for its replacement. It is confidently expected that their efforts will shortly be successful.* Our walk keeps on along the track (ignore the Private notice – this is a permissive path). It ends at an anglers' car-park. Keep straight on along the right hand edge of the field. At the end of the hedge on the right the path bends right and crosses the field to the flood bank of the River Nidd.

Turn left along the top of the flood bank and follow it until on a right hand curve you will see a wooden kissing-gate below you on the left. Go through and follow the path to the right of three massive oak trees, then keep straight across the middle of the field. At the far side the path bends right for a few yards then goes through another kissing-gate in the hedge on the left. Bear half right over the next field to the far right hand corner to yet another kissing-gate beside a large metal gate. This leads into a hedged track, which bears right and in a short distance turns left, now with a metalled surface.

Follow this track to a tarmac lane (Ness Lane once more) and turn left for 80 yards, then go through a gap in the hedge on the right (just to the right of a broad gateway) and follow the path almost round three sides of the field to where it turns left through the hedge into an enclosed path. Where this ends, keep forward to reach the road junction in the centre of Tockwith.

13. THE NIDD GORGE

6 miles (9 km) linear, 3½ miles (5½ km) circular. Explorer 289 Leeds. This is an interesting and varied walk with attractive views. It makes a very convenient half day linear walk, starting at Harrogate Railway Station or Bus Station (they are adjacent), and finishing at Knaresborough Railway Station or Bus Station. If a circular walk is preferred, you can start and finish at the car park close to the Gardeners Arms on Bilton Lane. The well-hidden Nidd Gorge is a delightful place, an extensive, steep-sided, wooded valley, at the bottom of which is the fast flowing River Nidd. Parts of the path through the gorge (particularly at the Knaresborough end) are very muddy in winter.

Turn right from the Harrogate Railway Station/Bus Station and continue to the bottom of Station Parade. Go straight across on to Mayfield Grove, then soon turn right on to Strawberry Dale, then left along Nydd Vale Terrace, a pleasant urban path beside the railway. Cross the pedestrian bridge over the railway, turn right for a short distance along Dragon Road, then turn right into Asda car park. Keep right (signposted Dragon Cycleway) and soon you come to a tarmac path/cycleway that goes under the bridge you have just crossed.

The path continues beside the railway and under the Skipton Road bridge, before climbing up to Grove Park Avenue Keep in the same direction for a short distance, then turn left across the green bridge over the railway. Turn right immediately after the bridge, keep right at the T-junction in a few yards and right again shortly afterwards when the path forks. You are now on the route of the former Harrogate to Ripon railway line. Ignore all paths to left and right. Hawthorn and other trees have grown to produce an attractive scene and there is lots of birdlife. After a considerable distance the path is joined from the right by the former line from Starbeck (this was the route of the Leeds-Thirsk line that missed Harrogate altogether), and soon you come out on to Bilton Lane at a small car park. Start here if you prefer the circular walk.

Turn right along Bilton Lane, and then left just before the Gardeners Arms down a lane (signposted "Footpath and Bridleway Nidd Gorge"). The path goes through a footpath gate to the right of Woodside Farm, and then reaches open country with good views westward towards Nidderdale. It then becomes an attractive enclosed path before dropping steeply into the wooded Nidd Gorge. Turn right at the signpost (Milners Fork) on the path to Knaresborough. When the path forks, take either route – they soon reunite.

The enjoyable path keeps close to the River Nidd for some considerable distance. At one point there is a particularly attractive grassy area. At another the path climbs high above the river by duckboard steps. At a fork keep left on the broader, descending path, which brings you back to the river. When a bridge is reached (the path up to Scotton), do not cross, and

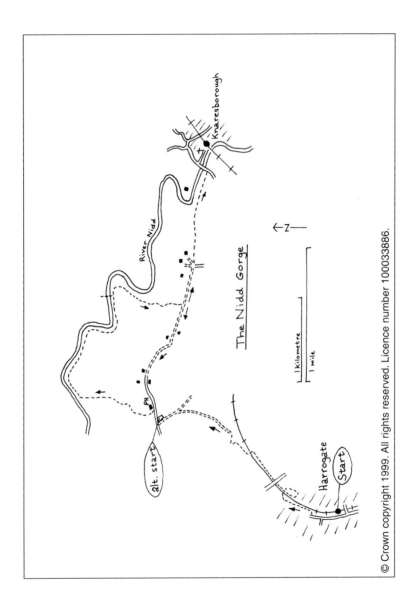

42

continue to keep the river on the left. Not long after, at a bench, the path starts to climb by steps up the hillside, and it is quite steep in places. Near the top keep left at the path junction. The path then continues along the top of the gorge for some distance, and this is where it can be extremely muddy in winter.

The path broadens to a track which leads to a tarmac lane. This is Bilton Lane: turn left (for the circular walk, turn right, and it is a straightforward walk back to the Gardeners Arms). Continue along the lane till you reach a junction at the entrance to Bilton Hall. Keep straight on here, along a firm path (signposted the Harrogate Ringway) which is also a cycle path, the Beryl Burton Way, named after the famous Yorkshire cyclist. There are good views of Knaresborough ahead, and the keep of the castle and the spire of Holy Trinity church are prominent. Later on as the path descends, you can see (well to the left of the castle), the diminutive stone tower of Knaresborough's much older parish church of St John.

Having gone through a kissing-gate beside a cattle grid, you reach a path junction. Leave the cycleway here (it bends right) and keep straight on along the Ringway path. At a fork by a signpost saying Conyngham Trail keep right, and at another junction you re-join the cycleway. Bear right over the bridge, then keep straight on along the tarmac path. Soon the Nidd is once more close by on the left. You pass an interesting and detailed information board about the Nidd Gorge and reach the main Harrogate to Knaresborough road beside the Yorkshire Lass pub.

There is a bus stop opposite the pub for those in a hurry to get back to Harrogate. Otherwise turn left and cross the bridge over the Nidd (known as the High Bridge), then turn right along Waterside. Turn left up Water Bag Bank, past the parish church *(its Slingsby monuments are famous)* to the railway station (carry straight on up Kirkgate for the town centre and bus station). Instead of going up Water Bag Lane, you can continue along Waterside and climb up the steps to the castle (destroyed in the Civil War, but the site is splendid and the remains quite substantial). The town centre and bus station are close to the castle.

14. STAVELEY and COPGROVE

6 miles (9½ km). Explorer 299 Ripon & Boroughbridge. This walk explores attractive undulating countryside with wide views. Staveley Nature Reserve, with its ponds, visited towards the end of the walk, is a particular attraction. There is a public hide, so you might like to bring binoculars.

Park off-road in Staveley in front of the Royal Oak near the church. Cars may also be parked on the main road near the triangular green. Bus no. 56/57 Harrogate-Knaresborough-Boroughbridge/Ripon (irregular times).

Walk past the church along the pleasant tree-lined road soon with a view of the former Staveley Corn Mill on the right. Keep left along the Knaresborough road at the road junction, then in a short distance turn left at the footpath sign and follow a farm track which climbs gently through an extensive field. There are good views at the top including both the North York Moors and the Pennines. Descend to the bottom of the hill, and go through a gap in the hedge on the right by a waymark (easy to miss). Keep to the hedge on the left, go through another gap in the hedge ahead, and then turn sharp right and follow the left side of the hedge up the hill. In the top corner of the field go through the gap in the hedge on the right, then turn left, now with the hedge on your left. When the road is reached, turn right along it past the houses of Occaney.

Turn left at the road junction (signposted Copgrove, Burton Leonard), and then just after the Occaney Beck is crossed (it used to be a ford), turn left along a signposted lane. Ignore a track forking off left and go through a gateway. The lane passes to the left of Walkingham Hill Farm. A short distance after the farm keep left at the fork (spinney on the left), and descend between high hedges to a metal gate and junction of paths by a signpost. Turn right on a broad track which climbs the wooded hillside beside an old limestone wall *(you are now on the magnesian limestone belt)* and then levels out. Keep in the same direction when the track is joined by a metalled road. Turn right through a bridleway gate (no sign) just before a wood on the right and follow the hedged track beside the wood. When the road is reached, turn left for a few yards to enjoy the view across the lake to Copgrove Hall *(built in the late 18th-century and ascribed to the York architect John Carr).*

Copgrove Hall

Retrace your steps, and continue along the road into Copgrove, ignoring the right turn to Knaresborough. When the road turns sharp right towards Staveley, continue straight on past a notice saying "Private Road No Entry" (there is a concealed bridleway sign!) and along a pleasant, quiet lane with good views. Ignore a track forking left over a cattle-grid, with a small wood on the right – Kilburn White Horse is soon clearly visible – and follow the lane until you pass round a barrier and to the left of a red-brick house, Roecliffe Lodge.

A few yards beyond the house turn right along another track, a new right of way created in 2006. Pass round a barrier and follow the track to Newfields Farm. At the farm follow the track left and then right, keeping all the buildings on the right, then keep straight on towards the next farm. Pass round a gate and follow the track along the field edge. About 40 yards before Carr Top Farm fork right along a path into the adjacent field.

The right of way used to bear left to follow the fence on your left as it bends right to a footbridge, and that still seems the sensible route. But strictly speaking you now have to walk forward over the narrow neck of field, then turn left to follow the field edge along to the bridge. Cross the bridge and enter the Yorkshire Wildlife Trust's Staveley Nature Reserve, Follow the clear path forward. You will reach the sturdy public hide, which gives a good view over one of the ponds. The next hide is for members only and is locked. Shortly after it there is an information board about the reserve. Pass through the kissing-gate and follow the woodland path to another kissing-gate, where you leave the Nature Reserve. The path becomes a track and leads to the Minskip Road. Turn right to return to the start of the walk.

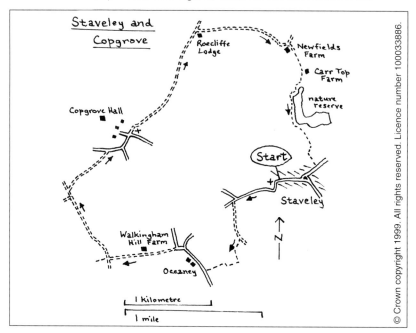

15. BOROUGHBRIDGE AND ALDBOROUGH

4¾ miles (7½ km). Explorer 299 Ripon & Boroughbridge. Boroughbridge and Aldborough, a few miles to the north east of Harrogate and Knaresborough, are places of great interest and antiquity, and well worth a look round. The route of the walk visits the major sites and takes in several other features of interest. Though there is quite a lot of road walking, the interest of the places visited makes it well worth the effort, and included in the route is a very pleasant riverside path.

The walk starts at the main (Back Lane) car-park in Boroughbridge (free) just beyond Hall Square (GR 397668) where there are toilets. There is a bus service to Boroughbridge from Harrogate and Knaresborough every 2 hours.

Leave the car park, walk straight along past Hall Square (TIC), and bear right into Fishergate, then turn right by the Crown Hotel (a former coaching inn) and along Bridge Street which used to be part of the Great North Road until the Boroughbridge by-pass was built in 1963. *Boroughbridge once had 22 inns.* Cross the fine bridge over the River Ure deep below, then shortly after this you cross the bridge over the Milby Cut, the navigable canal that avoids the rapids of Boroughbridge. *The River Ure was made navigable as far as Ripon around 1770, and there are cuts and six locks.* There is a pleasant walk upstream beside the cut and the river if you want to do an extra few hundred yards.

Retrace your steps into Boroughbridge. *Note the stone plaque in the middle of the bridge saying that the downstream side of the bridge dates from 1562, the upstream side from 1784, and that it was widened and reconstructed in 1949. At the Boroughbridge end of the bridge is another plaque, this time commemorating the Battle of Boroughbridge 1322, fought at the then wooden bridge when Edward II's army defeated the rebel forces of the Earls of Lancaster and Hereford.*

Retrace your steps along Bridge Street and continue straight on for a few yards after the Fishergate turn along Horsefair. Immediately after Golden Bite Fish and Chips turn right along Valuation Lane. The lane turns left, then right, and shortly after this there is a footpath on the left into a housing estate. After a short distance the footpath leads to a street which leads to a T-junction. Cross the road and turn left, then take the next street on the right. Bear right at the end, then continue along the tarmac footpath, which in a few yards turns left. At the next street turn right. At the fork keep left, but in a yard or two turn right to pass to the left of two garages (no footpath sign). The path turns left and leads to a tarmac road at the left side of an arable field. Turn left along the road.

Two of the Devil's Arrows are visible on the right at the far side of the field. At the T-junction cross diagonally right to the third of the Devil's Arrows. *It has a plaque which says "The Devil's Arrows three prehistoric monoliths of* millstone grit probably transported here from the area of Knaresborough c 2700 BC". The arrows are immensely impressive. The tallest is over 22 foot high and taller than any of the Stonehenge stones. The next tallest is scarcely less high, and the third one is 18 foot (and much broader than the others). They all have several vertical incisions at the top. There used to be a fourth but it is now part of the bridge over the River Tutt. To bring them from Knaresborough in c 2700 BC must have been a tremendous collective task. It is a pity perhaps that Boroughbridge doesn't display them to better effect; they are among the most impressive prehistoric monuments in England.

Go along the road towards Boroughbridge (i.e away from the nearby A1(M) which is very visible) passing Arrows Crescent and Druids Meadow en route. Turn left for a few yards along Horsefair *(the name indicates another*

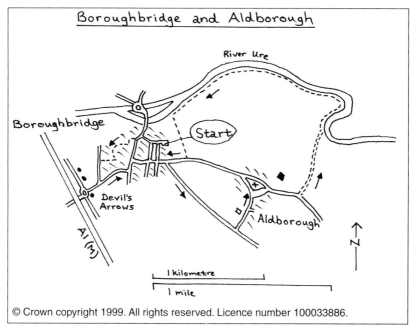

Boroughbridge and Aldborough

© Crown copyright 1999. All rights reserved. Licence number 100033886.

element of the town's history), then cross at the crossing and turn right into the first street (no name) and continue to St James Square: en route you cross the River Tutt. Keep straight on when St James Square is reached, but cross the road to look at the centrepiece of the square, a splendid octagonal roofed pump given by Mrs Lawson of Aldborough Manor in 1875. Its well is 256 feet deep. A short distance after the square, turn right along B6265 which is signposted to York and continue along it for half a mile to the crossroads at the top of the hill. There is a pavement throughout and for part of the way there is woodland on the left.

47

Turn left at the crossroads and descend the lane into Aldborough. There are fine Scots pine trees. *Shortly, on the left, you come to the entrance to the remains of the Roman town, Isurium Brigantium. The site, which has mosaic floors, is owned by English Heritage, and is open in April to June and September at weekends, in July and August from Thursday to Monday. Aldborough was quite an important place in Roman times, and was where the road from Ribchester in Lancashire and Ilkley joined the important route from York to the north. Today, it is an attractive village with many pantiled roofed houses.*

Continue down the road into the village and soon the delightful village green is reached with a maypole in the middle. You are going to leave the green in the bottom left hand corner, *but first turn right to the stocks and a diminutive building with a plaque saying that it is "The Old Court House of the Ancient borough of Aldborough and Boroughbridge of which members of Parliament were elected till 1832". The Reform Act of 1832 abolished the parliamentary seats of small towns (many of which were "rotten" or "pocket" boroughs), and redistributed them to larger centres of population.*

Now walk down to the bottom left hand corner of the green, where a short track leads to St. Andrew's Church, *built in a large and ancient burial ground in the heart of the Roman town, possibly on the site of a temple of Mercury (there is a Roman altar with a statue of the god inside). The present church was built c.1330, after the Norman one had been destroyed by the Scots in 1318, but the tower (built using stones from the Roman walls) and chancel are 15th-century. Inside is a fine large 14th-century brass of William de Aldeburgh.*

Walk round the church to the other (north) side and leave by a gate onto a road. *Along to the left you can see the tall stone Battle Cross, commemorating the battle in 1318, which used to stand in the Market Place in Boroughbridge.* Turn right along the road past the Ship Inn and follow it past a fine yew hedge beyond which is Aldborough Hall This road is on the line of the Roman Road to York.

Turn left at the end of the yew hedge along a narrow lane which leads to the River Ure. There is a view from it of Aldborough Hall. At the end of the track bear left up onto the flood bank and keep straight on along it. *This is where Aldborough's port would have been situated, but there are no obvious remains.*

Follow the path on the flood bank for about 1¼ miles. Can you spot the White Horse of Kilburn? You are likely to pass anglers, as the Ure is noted for its coarse fishing. After a time you will see the lock where the canal leaves the river and goes along Milby Cut. When you are faced by a fence across the flood bank, the path bears left away from the river and cuts across to Aldborough Road on the edge of Boroughbridge. Turn right, and St James Square is soon reached. Immediately before the square is reached, Back Lane on the right leads down to the car park.

16. BURTON LEONARD and BISHOP MONKTON

3¾ miles/6 km. Explorer 299 Ripon & Boroughbridge. An easy, flat walk across the fields. Route finding needs close attention on the first section.

Bus Harrogate-Burton Leonard. Park in the village by the lower green, the one with the shelter, parish pump and attractive stone map of the village.

Walk up the hill, passing to the right of the higher green, but about half way up, just after Hill Rise Cottage, turn right along Peter Lane. When you reach a crossing of lanes, turn left (signposted Sports Field), but soon the track turns sharp right again. Follow it past the tennis courts and bowling green, after which it turns sharp left again, and by the building housing the cricket scoreboard right again, following a hedge on the right. Enter a short stretch with hedges on both sides to reach a large field. Cross it diagonally left, heading towards power lines in the distance and a clump of trees some way left of a pylon.

After a time you will notice that you are making for a white post behind the hedge. Go through the gap in the hedge beside the post and walk straight across the corner of the next field towards a pylon beyond the next hedge. There is another white post concealed in the hedge. Cross the stile and walk diagonally right over the next field to the next stile, then keep the same line over the next field, passing to the left of the pylon, to the left hand end of the hedge in front. Pass the end of the hedge and bear slightly left over the next field, heading for a post to the right of and some way in front of a small clump of trees. At the post bear right and make for a fence corner. Walk along with the fence on your left to reach a cross track. This is Mains Lane. Wormald Green is to the left, but we turn right. Navigational problems are now over!

At the end of this field the track forks in front of an open barn: keep left, to follow a hedge on the left. At the end of this field pass through a gateway into a hedged way. After passing a house, the track becomes tarmac. Follow it to a road on the edge of Bishop Monkton, cross it and turn right along the footway. When you reach the road junction by the church, the village centre is to the left along St. John's Road, but the walk continues to the right, along the access road to Church Farm. Here you join the Ripon Rowel Walk.

Pass the farm and bear left into the caravan site, and follow the hedge on the left. Keep forward to the end of the caravan park and cross the stile in the boundary fence. Walk straight across the field to a gate. Cross the stile beside it and walk straight across the next field to the next stile, after which you have a hedge on the left to the next stile. Walk straight over the middle of the next field to the next stile. Cross it and continue straight across the next large, undulating field, passing close to a telegraph pole. Climb the bank, pass under two sets of overhead wires and make for a stile in the top right hand corner of the field.

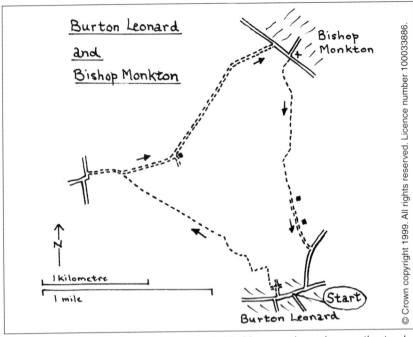

Follow the farm track across the next field. After passing a house, the track becomes tarmac. Having passed some more houses, you reach a narrow lane: turn right along it, and at the T-junction by the church turn right to return to your starting point.

LONGER WALKS AROUND HARROGATE

As you follow the routes described in this book, you will come across signposts indicating that you are on the Harrogate Ringway or the Knaresborough Round. Each of these is an attractive, varied 21-mile circular walk, around Harrogate in the one case and Knaresborough in the other. The route of the Harrogate Ringway is well provided with public transport, so can easily be walked in sections, and the Knaresborough Round can be divided into two sections using the bus service that runs via Ferrensby. With the aid of the OS maps shorter circular walks based on these two longer walks can easily be devised.

For leaflets about these walks send a SAE with 30 pence to P.L. Goldsmith, 20 Pannal Ash Grove, Harrogate, HG2 0HZ

50

17. SOUTH STAINLEY, BURTON LEONARD and BREARTON

7 miles/11 km or 3 miles/5 km. Explorer 299 Ripon & Boroughbridge. Field paths and unmetalled rural lanes that offer fine views across this area of fertile unspoilt countryside. Much of the walk is in the Mountgarret Estate.

Harrogate-Ripon bus to South Stainley (Red Lion Inn). Church car-park at the end of the village (not Sunday mornings).

From the bus stop walk down the village lane and cross Stainley Beck to St. Wilfrid's church *(built in 1845)*. Cross the stile by the gate into the field alongside the churchyard and follow the wall on your left. At the end of the wall cross another stile and keep forward across the next field parallel to the fence on the left. Go through a gap in the next hedge and keep the same line to a stile in the corner of the next field. Follow the right hand edge of the next field, with a wood on the right. The wood ends at the next stile: cross, walk forward and keep the hedge on the left in the next field.

In the next field you join a good track: keep forward along it. At the end of this field ignore the track forking left. At the end of the next field the track bends right, then turns left through the hedge. Now the field boundary is on your right. At the end of this field cross the beck. Looking straight ahead, you will see a power line pole with a yellow waymark arrow. Cross the corner of the field to this pole, then with your back to the pole cross the next field diagonally left, heading just to the left of a tall tree seen beyond the far hedge with a white notice visible to the right of it. Go through a gap in the hedge and follow the clear path up to a track coming through a gate on the right. Turn left and follow the broad track uphill. Leave the plantation and continue up the left hand edge of the field. At the top of the hill the houses of Burton Leonard appear ahead. Follow the field edge to the village.

When you reach the road, turn right along it and follow it down to the junction, where there is a bench. Turn right – this is Limekiln Lane. When the track forks, you can either take the right hand branch and continue down the lane, or go left to walk through Burton Leonard Lime Quarries Nature Reserve, which is worth visiting for the flowers, especially in spring. If you choose this latter option, you will reach another fork, where you can either go right to rejoin the lane or keep left through the reserve. At the next fork, if you go left you can visit the old quarry, but you will need to return to this point to resume the walk, for the path straight ahead leads back to the lane at Lime Kilns Cottage. Bear left along the lane. Cross the beck by the footbridge at Lime Kilns Farm and continue to the top of the rise. Look back for an attractive view of the ford and the farm beyond *(the front cover picture of this book)*.

At the top you have a choice of either returning directly by the shorter route 'A' or continuing your walk towards Brearton along route 'B'.

South Stainley, Burton Leonard and Brearton

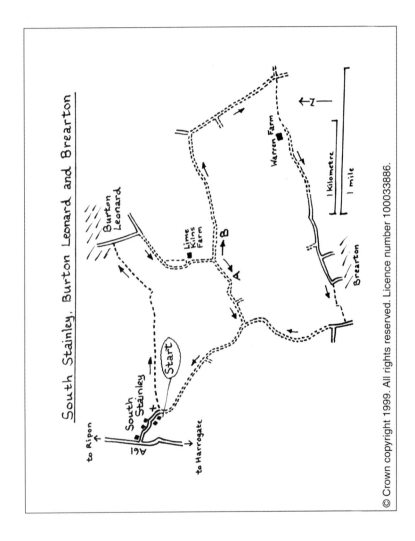

A. Turn right along the rural lane, ignore a track forking left, pass a wood on the left, ignore a signposted bridleway coming in from the left, and at the

next junction, with an old boundary stone on the left, turn right, here rejoining the longer walk. The lane meanders downhill, passes Stainley Hall over to the right and continues across the old stone bridge spanning Stainley Beck. Turn left at the junction to return to the village.

'B' Turn left along the track. A short way along ignore a track forking right into a field. Follow your track to a T-junction with the end of a tarmac lane across Robert Beck on your left. Turn right up the track. Towards the top of the hill the surface becomes tarmac. A little further on, where this lane turns right, keep straight on along the green lane, which eventually drops downhill beside Warren Covert with an old wall on the right. At the foot of the hill cross the stile by the gate on the right and walk straight across the large field towards Warren Farm in the distance. Shortly before you reach the hedge at the end of the field, bear slightly left under the telegraph wires to a bridle gate into a fenced track.

Pass the entrance to Warren Farm and follow the tarmac lane. Pass the driveway to Hill Top Farm, keep straight on at the road junction (the village of Brearton is along to the left), and when the lane turns left, cross the stile on the right and follow the left hand edge of the field along. Cross the next stile and keep forward for 10 yards to the next stile on the left. Cross and turn right, now with the hedge on the right. At the end of the field turn left with the hedge to find a stile on the right in front of a large tree. Cross and walk forward to the right of the old hedgerow, then continue to the right of the hedge ahead to a stile by a gate onto a road.

Turn right along the road and when it turns left continue straight ahead along a lane bordering a wood on the left. Eventually you reach a T-junction with an old boundary stone on the right. Turning left, join the shorter walk, as the lane meanders downhill, passes Stainley Hall over to the right and continues across the old stone bridge spanning Stainley Beck. Turn left at the junction to return to the village.

18. SOUTH STAINLEY to CAYTON and MARKINGTON

6¼ miles/10 km. Explorer 299 Ripon & Boroughbridge. An easy circuit, mainly on tracks, though pleasant countryside. The lane from Markington can be exceedingly wet and muddy.

Harrogate-Ripon bus to South Stainley (Red Lion Inn). Church car-park at the end of the village (not Sunday mornings).

From the bus stop walk down the village lane and cross Stainley Beck to St. Wilfrid's church (built in 1845). Continue along the lane, and when you reach a fork, keep right over the bridge. Pass the approach drive to Stainley Hall on the left and shortly afterwards, where the lane begins to climb, fork right along a track. Cross a cattle-grid and ignore a track forking right. Cross another cattle-grid, enter a hedged lane, pass Green Lane Farm and follow the access road to a minor road. Bear right along this to the A61, crossing the former Ripon-Harrogate railway line.

Cross the busy main road with care, climb the bank and turn left along the broad verge. Take the first track on the right (bridleway sign). Immediately after passing a wood on the left go through a bridle gate on the left and follow the hedge on the left to another bridle gate at Cayton Grange Farm. Go through and immediately turn right, over a cattle-grid and up a good track with a hedge on the right. After a time the track runs between a fence and a hedge. When you reach a junction, keep straight on. Pass Falls Wood on the left and continue along the track to reach a T-junction.

Turning right here would be a short cut back to South Stainley, but the walk continues by turning left. When you reach High Cayton Farm, turn sharp right on a less clear track, and when it soon bears left towards a hedge, leave it, to keep straight on on a less distinct track. Pass under the power lines, pass the end of a hedge on the right, go through a gate – Hincks' Wood is over to the right – and follow the hedge on the left (no clear path). At the end of the field turn right with the hedge for a short distance, then turn left through a gate and continue once more by the hedge on the left, again on a track.

Follow the track to Hincks' Hall Farm, bear left to pass between the buildings and follow the farm access track to Markington. Where the track makes a sharp bend to the right, the bridleway keeps straight on, down through trees. Follow it the short distance to the road and turn right through Markington. At the crossroads the village centre with the Yorkshire Hussar pub is straight ahead, but the walk turns right. Here you join the Ripon Rowel Walk. When the road bends right, keep straight ahead up a lane. The lane becomes a track. In a short distance ignore a footpath forking off left: keep on the track.

When the track turns sharp left to pass through a gate, go through the left hand of the two gates in front of you and follow the hedge on the right.

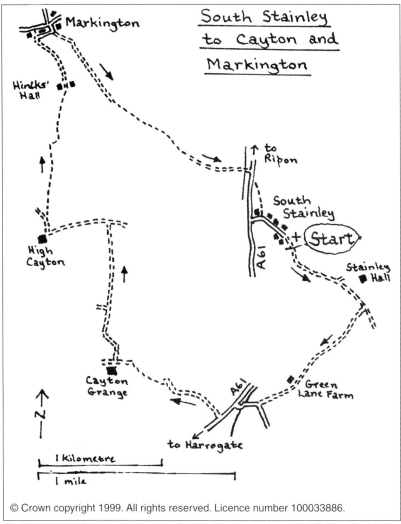

South Stainley
to Cayton and
Markington

Markington

Hincks' Hall

to Ripon

South Stainley

+ Start

High Cayton

A61

Stainley Hall

Cayton Grange

Green Lane Farm

A61

N

to Harrogate

1 Kilometre

1 mile

Traffic on the A61 can once again be heard. At the end of this field cross the ditch into the next one, bear left, then follow the field edge which curves to the right. Soon you are on a track between field boundaries. Follow this track to the A61, crossing the former railway line once more just before you reach it. Turn right along the verge for 70 yards, then cross the road and go through the gap in the hedge with a pylon beyond. Walk diagonally right across the field to a hedge corner, some way to the right of the houses, and follow the hedge along to a road. Turn right for the bus stop, left to return to the car-park.

19. RIPLEY TO RIPON VIA MARKINGTON AND MARKENFIELD HALL

8½ miles (13½ km). Explorer 299 Ripon & Boroughbridge. A linear walk through pastoral scenery, passing Markenfield Hall. The Hall, which dates from the early 14th century, with Elizabethan and later alterations, presents a remarkable example of a fortified and moated manor house. Harrogate-Ripon bus to Ripley. There is a large free car-park at the entrance to Ripley village off the A61 Harrogate-Ripon road.

Walk through the village in the Ripon direction, passing the cobbled square, stocks and Boar's Head on the left and the Hôtel de Ville on the right. Towards the end of the village fork left through a gateway with an old milestone on the right (Pateley Bridge 9½) along a stretch of disused road. At the main road to Pateley Bridge cross straight over into the minor road opposite (Birthwaite Lane). After some considerable distance when the road bends left, fork right off it along a track. Cross a cattle-grid and keep left at the next fork.

Pass through a gate at the corner of a wood and continue along the track with the wood on your right. The track reaches a fork: the left branch passes through a gate, but you keep right, down to a couple of seats with a fine view to the Kilburn White Horse and the North York Moors. Now continue downhill on the track. At the foot go through the gate into the field and follow the track as it first bends left along the field edge, then just before the field corner turns right, crosses a beck, passes through a gate and follows the left hand edge of the next field up towards Cayton Gill Farm.

Much new tree planting has taken place around here. Pass through the gateway out of the field and bear half left with a fence at first on the right and soon on both sides. The fenced path ends at a gateway: go through and walk straight downhill to a gate. Keep forward across the dip, then bear half left across a large field. The clear path soon leads along the bottom of a bank and eventually reaches a wood. Turn right through the gate and walk up to a bridle gate then straight across the field to High Cayton Farm. Pass through two gates and walk through the farm, passing the farmhouse on the right.

At a junction of tracks turn left, but when the track soon bears left towards a hedge, leave it, to keep straight on on a less distinct track. Pass under the power lines, pass the end of a hedge on the right, go through a gate – Hincks' Wood is over to the right – and follow the hedge on the left (no clear path). At the end of the field turn right with the hedge for a short distance, then turn left through a gate and continue once more by the hedge on the left, again on a track.

Follow the track to Hincks' Hall Farm, bear left to pass between the buildings and follow the farm access track to Markington. Where the track makes a sharp bend to the right, the bridleway keeps straight on, down

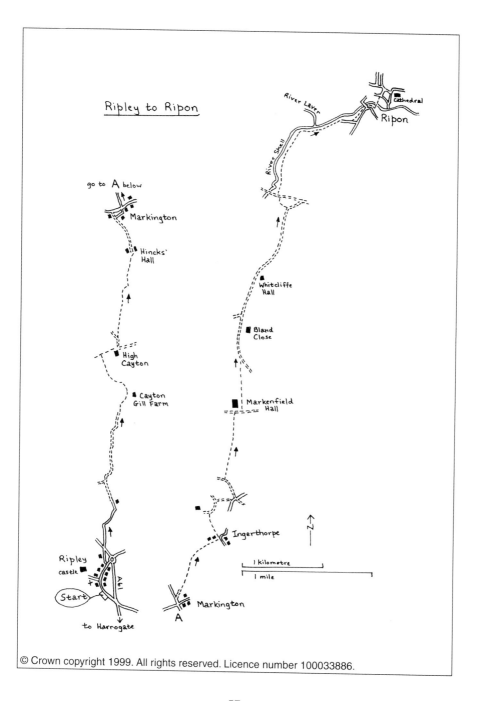

through trees. Follow it the short distance to the road and turn right through Markington. At the crossroads the village centre with the Yorkshire Hussar pub is straight ahead, but the walk turns left (Westerns Lane), crosses the bridge and forks right along a track. (For the next 2½ miles the route coincides with the Ripon Rowel Walk with its 6-point circular logo waymarks.) Pass a cottage and go through a kissing-gate into the cricket field, and bear left round the boundary, passing the pavilion, to reach another gate on the left.

Go through, immediately turn left into the next field, then immediately right again, to follow the fence on the right. When it turns right, go with it, then behind the goalposts turn left again to follow another hedge on the left to another kissing-gate. Bear left, passing to the left of two solitary trees, after which you are on a track which leads to the hamlet of Ingerthorpe. The track leads through a gate. Walk half-left the few yards to a smaller gate, then along a gravel drive, and just as you reach the road, turn left along a footpath.

Cross a stile and follow the hollow way uphill, then continue along the woodland path to a stile and a narrow lane. Turn right. At a junction ignore a track forking left and follow the tarmac lane to a junction. Turn left and in a few yards left again along a track. When the main track turns left through a large double gate, keep forward into a small wood. At the end of the wood cross a stile by a gate on the right and walk straight across the field into a broad fenced track. Where this ends, keep on by the fence on the right and when the fence ends at a wall, keep straight over the next field towards Markenfield Hall.

Go through a large gate and turn right through the farmyard and onto a tarmac lane. At the end of the buildings go through the gate on the left. (At this point it is possible to shorten your walk by continuing along the drive to the A61 and catching a bus back to Ripley.) Walk up the left hand edge of the field. A step-stile in the wall on the left

Markenfield Hall

gives access to the front of the hall, certainly worth a look, although there is no right of way. The public footpath continues up the field, passing the side of the hall and following the fence along to a stile by a gate, then keep forward by a fence on the right. When the fence bends right, keep straight forward over the field, heading for the right hand corner of the wood.

Here you will find a stile in the fence. Cross it and the sleeper footbridge and turn left to find a step-stile in the wall on the right. Cross it and turn left along the track. In the next two fields follow the hedge on the left, passing Bland Close Farm over to the right. Join the farm access track and keep forward along it. In a short distance Whitcliffe Lane comes in from the left. Keep forward along the tarmac lane, (soon Ripon Cathedral comes into view, with the Kilburn White Horse and the North York Moors beyond) and follow it until you reach the far end of a wood on the left. Turn left into the field and follow its left hand edge as it bears right down to Hell Wath Cottage. Turn left down the lane. At the bottom have a look at the information panel about the Sanctuary Marker Way on the left before turning right along the track into the trees.

Keep to the main track, which soon emerges from the wood and crosses open ground to the river bank. Follow the river along. Shortly after descending a flight of concrete steps you reach a footbridge at the confluence of the Rivers Skell and Laver. Keep forward along the riverside path, which becomes a track and eventually a tarmac road. Just before this reaches the main road, go through a gate on the left into a children's play area and cross it to a gate on the far side. Steps over to the right lead up to the main road and bus stops, but to continue the walk to the centre of Ripon keep on by the river, passing through the tunnel under the main road to join another road. Turn left along this, but cross the Skell by the next bridge (Williamson Drive) and walk through the residential development. Just after a car-park on the left turn left along a tarmac footpath and follow it to the next road (Water Skellgate). Turn right to the junction, then cross the road and walk up Duck Hill to the Market Place. Walk along the right hand edge of this, turning right through The Arcade. At the end, the bus station is a short distance to the left.

20. RIPON TO STUDLEY PARK

6¼ miles (10 km). Explorer 299 Ripon & Boroughbridge. An easy stroll from Ripon to Fountains Abbey, taking in the deer park and the Valley of the Seven Bridges. The walk starts at the west door of Ripon Cathedral. Park in one of the town centre car-parks. Bus Harrogate-Ripon.

From the west door of the cathedral cross the main road and walk forward along Kirkgate. Where it bends right, go down the steps on the left, cross the road and turn left to the junction with Water Skellgate. Cross diagonally right (care, busy road!) then bear left between the bollards onto a tarmac footpath. At the end turn right, follow the street as it bends left, pass through the residential development and cross the River Skell by the bridge. Turn right along the footway for 50 yards, then fork right along the path by the river which leads under the main Ripon-Harrogate road. Walk through the children's play area, out the other side and turn right.

At the end of the road keep forward along the track with the river close by on the right. Cross the river by the first footbridge, at the confluence of the Laver and the Skell, and follow the tarmac path, forking left to follow the Laver to the next road. Turn left, but immediately fork left again to follow a short woodland path. At the far end this leads back onto the road. Turn left. At the road junction turn left on the Pateley Bridge road, crossing to the footway on the other side and crossing the River Laver by Bishopton Bridge. A few yards after the entrance to the River Laver Holiday Park cross the road again and go through a kissing-gate opposite.

Follow the hedged path across the fields, keeping straight on when you reach a crossing of paths. Cross straight over the main street of Studley Roger and continue along the path opposite. Go through a kissing-gate and across a field to the next kissing-gate leading into the deer park. Bear slightly left across the grass. *The park, which is well stocked with herds of Red, Manchurian Sika and the smaller Fallow deer, is enhanced by many indigenous and foreign trees planted during the 18th century by John*

Aislabie, a former Chancellor of the Exchequer. When you reach the main avenue leading up to St. Mary's Church (1871), bear right up it. Take the first road forking left, signposted Lakeside car-park.

Where the road bends right to pass along by the lake to the National

In the Valley of Seven Bridges

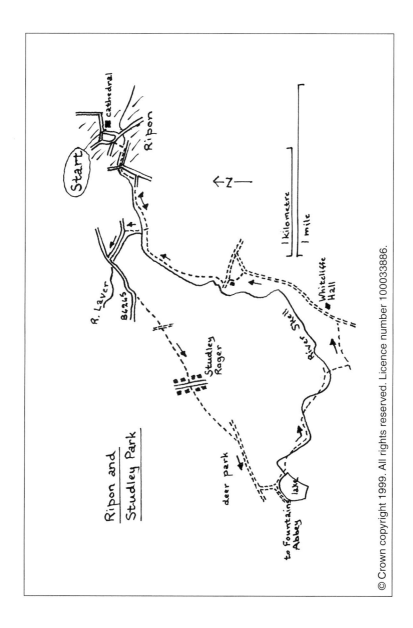

Ripon and Studley Park

Start

cathedral ■ Ripon

Ripon

R. Laver

B4245

Studley Roger

deer park

River Skell

Whitcliffe Hall ■

to Fountains Abbey

lake

←Z→

1 kilometre
1 mile

Trust car-park and the entrance to Fountains Abbey, fork left off it along a stony track which passes to the left of the bottom of the lake and crosses the Skell outflow by a footbridge. Turn left, and where the track forks keep left, heading for the first of the little stone bridges over the river. As you approach the second bridge, look up to the left, where you will see on the bluff a small stone building, the Devil's Chimney. After the fifth bridge you pass through a gate and leave the deer park.

Continue through Chinese Wood, before crossing the Skell once more by the footbridge a little further on. Go left for a few yards, then bear to the right uphill along a wide cart track, and then sharp left at the crossing near the top of the hill, where the main track turns to the right. Go through the gate and bear left, keeping to the right of a line of old hawthorn trees to reach Whitcliffe Lane. Turn left and follow the lane until you reach the far end of a wood on the left. Turn left into the field and follow its left hand edge as it bears right down to Hell Wath Cottage. Turn left along the lane and follow it down to the bottom. Have a look at the information panel about the Sanctuary Marker Way on the left before turning right along the track into the trees.

Keep to the main track, which soon emerges from the wood and crosses open ground to the river bank. Follow the river along. Shortly after descending a flight of concrete steps you reach the footbridge you crossed earlier. Keep forward to return to the start along your outward route.

Rambling around Ripon

The Ripon Group of the Ramblers' Association has published Rambles around Ripon, *a collection of 15 local walks ranging in length from 1½ to 9 miles, and a guide to the* Ripon Rowel Walk, *a 50-mile circular walk starting in Ripon and extending as far north as Masham and as far south as South Stainley, with 12 small circular walks en route.*

A leaflet is available from the Ripon TIC describing the Sanctuary Way Walk, *a 10-mile walk (with shorter possibilities). In 937 King Athelstan granted the right of Sanctuary as part of the Liberty of St. Wilfrid. The Sanctuary Boundary of the settlement in those days, within which anyone could be granted sanctuary overnight, was marked by eight Sanctuary markers. In 2005 local Rotary Clubs created and installed replica Sanctuary markers close to the original sites, and this walk links them. Interpretation boards have been set up along the route.*